Newbridge Discovery Links — Early Level

Teacher's Guide

Brenda Parkes

We would like to thank Ann Scholl, former
Executive Officer of Akron Ohio City Schools,
for her contributions in the development of
Discovery Links.

Newbridge Discovery Links Teacher's Guide
ISBN: 1-56784-080-9

Written by Brenda Parkes
Edited and Designed by Curriculum Concepts

Newbridge Educational Publishing
333 East 38 Street, New York, NY 10016
Copyright © 1999 Newbridge Educational Publishing, LLC
All rights reserved. No part of this publication may
be reproduced or transmitted in any form or by any
means, electronic or mechanical, including photocopy,
recording, or any information storage or retrieval system,
without permission in writing from the publisher.
Printed in the United States of America.

10 9 8 7 6 5 4 3 2

Table of Contents

Introduction

What Is Guided Reading?	5
Early Readers	5
Why Non-fiction Guided Reading?	6
Why a Science Focus?	6
Language Arts Standards	7
32 Titles Leveled into Two Sets	8
Non-fiction Features of Discovery Links Guided Reading Books	10
Overview of Teacher's Notes	14
Using the Teacher's Notes	14

Set A

Animals From Long Ago	17
Animal Messengers	20
At the Playground	23
Beaks	26
Bikes	29
City Buildings	32
Day and Night	35
How Animals Move	38
Kittens	41
Let's Make Something New	44
Rocks	47
Snails in School!	50
Up Close	53
What Can Change?	56
What Does a Garden Need?	59
Where Are the Eggs?	62

Set B

Animals Build	65
At the Science Center	68
The Coral Reef	71
Corn: From Farm to Table	74
From the Earth	77
Fur, Feathers, Scales, Skin	80
Let's Bake	83
Light and Shadow	86
Our Senses	89
Recycle It!	92
Sounds All Around	95
Stars	98
Taking Care of Baby	101
Watching the Weather	104
What Do Scientists Do?	107
Where Does the Water Go?	110

Credits

Photo Credits	113

Science Standards/Benchmarks

National Science Education Standards and Benchmarks for Science Literacy—Project 2061	114

About the Author

About the Author	120

Introduction

What Is Guided Reading?

Guided reading involves supporting a small group of students thinking, talking, and reading purposefully through a new text with guidance from the teacher. Grouping is dynamic and includes students who are at a similar developmental level and share needs and behaviors at a particular time.

The purpose of guided reading is to help children develop effective skills and strategies that they can use flexibly and appropriately to:

- comprehend what they read
- figure out unknown words
- read and understand new sentence structures

Through on-going observation and assessment, the teacher chooses books at increasing levels of challenge to:

- support children to use what they already know
- challenge children to learn and apply new skills and strategies

Early Readers

Early readers have control over a number of early strategies. They expect to get meaning from texts and are increasingly able to read selected texts independently after they have been provided with an appropriate introduction.

Although there will be variations among individuals depending on their experiences and capabilities, early readers generally:

- demonstrate increasing control of early reading strategies
- increasingly use strategies such as searching, checking, and self-correcting
- recognize a number of sight words
- rely less on pictures
- use more sources of information to read
- confirm by cross-checking to known items
- use letter/sound relationships to predict and check meaning

Why Non-fiction Guided Reading?

Research shows that 80% of the reading and writing we do every day is non-fiction. Non-fiction reading is also featured in all national testing. In this "age of information," it is vital that students understand how to gather, interpret, and communicate information. This process requires an understanding of:

- the different ways information can be read and communicated (for example, through photographs, diagrams, maps, charts, tables, and other forms of visual depictions)
- the specialized language and language structures used in non-fiction texts
- the way non-fiction is organized to highlight information
- the selective way non-fiction is read according to the reader's purpose

See pages 10 through 13 of this Guide for an outline of how non-fiction is presented in the program.

Why a Science Focus?

A science focus does many things:

- It relates to what students see and do in the real world.
- It presents the world through realistic photographs.
- It provides opportunities for students to actively engage in learning.
- It helps children view the world scientifically and realistically.
- It creates opportunities for students to ask and seek answers to questions by collecting, observing, organizing, classifying, comparing, contrasting, and communicating.
- It establishes continuity between a specific guided reading title and science-center displays and activities.

Language Arts Standards

Discovery Links books help children achieve the Language Arts Standards (the excerpts listed below have been extracted from the Compendium of Standards and Benchmarks for K–12 Education). These standards help ensure that the student:

- comprehends the main idea of simple expository information
- recognizes characteristic sounds and rhythms of language
- demonstrates a basic familiarity with selected non-fiction
- makes simple inferences regarding, "What will happen next...?"
- demonstrates competence in speaking and listening as tools for learning
- understands that reading is a way of gaining information about the world
- creates mental pictures for concrete information he or she has read
- uses picture clues and picture captions as aids to comprehension
- writes compositions that make effective use of very general, frequently used words to convey basic ideas
- demonstrates competence in the general skills and strategies of the writing process

32 Titles Leveled into Two Sets

Discovery Links books have been carefully developed to facilitate guided reading for early readers. The levels have been determined in consultation with a team of Reading Recovery teachers to provide a gradual increase in challenge.

Set A books provide:
- moderate-to-strong photo/text match
- consistent layouts
- varied opening and closing sentences
- repeated phrases
- variation in placement of text
- a variety of tenses

For example, in *Beaks*, children experience:
- repetitive language
- strong photo/text match

Set A

This is a flamingo.
Flamingos have big, curved beaks.

This is a hummingbird.
Hummingbirds have long, thin beaks.

In *Where Are the Eggs?*, children experience:
- variation of placement of type
- strong photo/text match

Where will this alligator lay her eggs?

Here they are.
They are in a nest on the ground, too.

The books in **Set B** introduce additional print and language features, such as:

- more complex sentence structures
- a number of different layouts
- a greater amount of written text
- specialized vocabulary
- less consistency and repetition in sentence patterns
- tables, charts, diagrams
- indexes, contents pages

For example, in *Light and Shadow*, children experience:
- more complex structures
- longer sentences

Set B

This boy's shadow is not flat. His shadow bends because the steps bend.

When something blocks out the light you can see its shadow.

In *Recycle It!*, children experience:
- specialized vocabulary
- different layouts

Plastic is recycled. These pails are made from recycled plastic.

These children are making new paper from old paper.

Non-fiction Features of Discovery Links Guided Reading Books

The books in this program have been designed to encourage and support children's use of the many features found in informational books. These features include:

- the organizational patterns and layout features that provide access to information, such as contents pages, indexes, and headings
- the specialized language and language structures of informational texts
- the use of photographs, charts, diagrams, tables, drawings, and other forms of visual literacy

Children will have many opportunities to use these features in reading and as powerful models for writing on topics relating to earth, life, and physical science.

All books are illustrated with superb photographs that support and extend the written language.

Take a look at a city.
You will see many buildings.

This building is made mostly of cement.

A babysitter takes care of these babies.
The sitter watches them while their parents search for food.

Non-fiction language and language structures are used throughout the titles.

Grandma cracks the eggs
into the bowl.
Then I mix it all together.

We add the flour, salt,
and baking powder.
Next we add the sugar and stir.

Specialized language is used in highly supportive contexts.

Sometimes you can see stars
in a group.
These groups are called clusters.

This is a cluster of stars.
It is called the Seven Sisters.

Headings provide focus for some titles.

Skin

Many animals have skin.
Elephants have thick skin.

Elephants eat leaves from trees.
The thick skin keeps them
from getting cut and scratched.

Contents pages are supported by pictograms at the A Level.

Indexes introduce children to the concept of looking up topics.

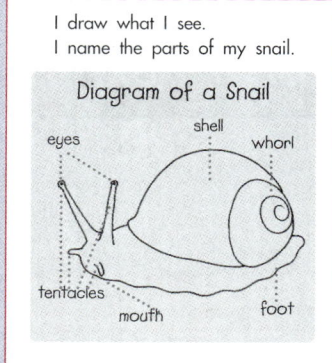

Labeled diagrams provide young readers with clear examples of this feature of informational texts.

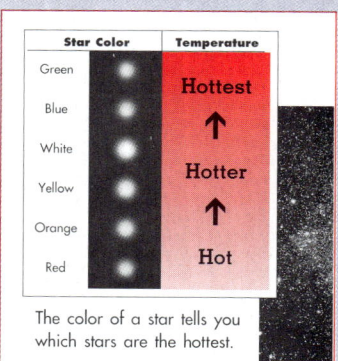

Every bike has many parts. How many parts can you name?

I draw what I see.
I name the parts of my snail.

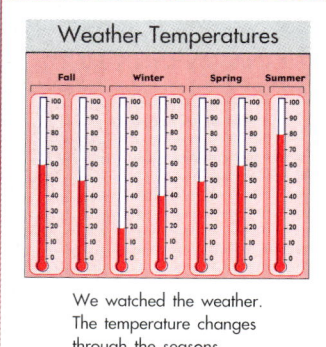

Charts model ways of presenting information through graphic organizers.

The color of a star tells you which stars are the hottest.

We watched the weather. The temperature changes through the seasons.

Procedures for activities and experiments are outlined in several books.

Dad makes two holes near the top of the bottle.

I put the string through the holes. We tie it.

The organizational pattern of comparison is used in some books.

This is a parrot.
Parrots have short, sharp beaks.

They use their beaks to open hard nuts.

This is a robin.
Robins have small, pointed beaks.

They use their beaks to catch worms.

Overview of Teacher's Notes

The teacher's notes for Discovery Links provide:

- important features built into each book that support guided reading
- a suggested sequence for talking, thinking, and reading through the book the first time
- suggestions for observing and prompting independent oral reading
- ideas for discussing the reading process and book content
- suggestions for science connections and cross-curricular activities
- suggestions for related non-fiction reading, fiction reading, writing activities, and science-center projects
- activities that encourage a home/school connection

These notes are intended as a guide to be used flexibly and appropriately according to the students' individual experiences, knowledge, and needs.

Using the Teacher's Notes

The teacher's notes for each of the 32 titles follow a consistent format. The following features are included for each title:

Standards and Benchmarks
Correlation to the National Science Education Standards and Benchmarks for Science Literacy—Project 2061

Supports
In this section you will find a list of features from the book that support the reader, such as language, clear text organization, and meaningful content.

Challenges
This bulleted list displays the features of the book that may challenge the reader, such as specialized vocabulary, words requiring closer attention to visual detail, variety of print placements, or a particular non-fiction feature.

Using the Teacher's Notes (continued)

Text features
This analysis highlights punctuation, high-frequency words, and letter/sound information. Although a number of features may appear in each book, only focus on those that have become important during the reading.

Introducing the text
The suggestions in this section link the reader's own experiences knowledge, and understanding with the concept explored in the text. The focus is on meaning. The suggestions relate directly to each book. However, if the concept is outside the experience of the group, the discussion may need to begin with a brief, concrete, hands-on exploration.

The first reading
The first reading should provide a framework for accessing the book and support independent problem-solving strategies.

Rereading and discussing
These notes offer suggestions for observing and supporting individual children as they read the book aloud. Possible discussion points are also included.

Science connections
These connections support and extend the concepts introduced in the Guided Reading books. Many are hands-on activities, providing children with opportunities to conduct experiments and perform real-life science activities.

Using the Teacher's Notes (continued)

Reading and writing science

Here you will find ideas for further investigations that relate to and extend the concepts in each book. *The emphasis is on gaining experience and enjoying science.* The activities involve independent as well as collaborative investigations and observations, and explorations with a variety of science tools, such as rulers, magnifiers, and charts. The instructions suggest ways to record and communicate information using the language and graphic organizers of non-fiction. If possible, include the activities in corresponding learning centers. Further enrichment ideas can be found in the *Newbridge Early Science Program*.

Cross-curricular activities

These activities provide opportunities to extend and enrich children's experiences across the curriculum in math, social studies, language arts, music, and art.

Home/school connections

These activities link the concept of each book to the wider world of home and community. They provide opportunities for children to continue observations and inquiries with their families and friends.

Non-fiction

This list will help you locate related books for inclusion in science and library centers. Children will be able to read some books on their own. Others are appropriate for reading to the class. And still others are resources that contain facts and ways to explore science with young children.

Fiction

This list will also help you locate related books for inclusion in your reading centers. As with the non-fiction, children will be able to read some books on their own, while others are appropriate for reading to the class.

Animals From Long Ago   Set A

Standards
Characteristics of organisms

Benchmarks
Some kinds of organisms that once lived on earth have completely disappeared although they were similiar to others that are alive today.

Supports
- repetitive text structure
- strong photo/drawing/text match

Challenges
- varied placement of text
- specialized vocabulary

Text features
Punctuation: apostrophe

High-frequency words: *have, long, old, their, these, like, some, ways, what*

Digraphs: *ph, th, wh*

Introducing the text
- Discuss the front- and back-cover photographs. Establish that these animals lived a long time ago and ask children to read the title. Talk about other animals that are extinct, what they looked like, and present-day animals that are like them in some ways.

The first reading

Title page: Read the page together and briefly discuss what information is given by the photographs.

Pages 2-3:   Ask: *What do you see here?* Discuss the photographs, modeling the written language as you do so. Ask children to find the words that tell how we can learn about animals from long ago.

Pages 4-5:   Have children use chunking, or putting letters together to make familiar "chunks," to confirm the word *mammoth*.

Pages 6-7:   Ask what the paintings show and have children read the answer. Model the language and language pattern on the next page.

Long ago, there were animals we don't see today.
Their prints are in old rock.

2

17

Pages 8-16: Continue this way, introducing each new animal and encouraging the children to use a variety of strategies to read their names and to recognize the repetitive pattern of information.

There are no dinosaurs now.

Observe children as they read their books aloud, but independently of each other. Are they using the text structure to anticipate meaning? Using phrasing? Self-correcting? Using a variety of effective strategies to maintain meaning?

Rereading and discussing

- Invite responses to the book. What interested them the most? What questions do they have about extinct animals? How could they answer their questions?
- Discuss the repetitive structure and the support it provided and comment positively on effective strategies you observed children using. Observe again as they read their book to themselves or a friend.
- Provide opportunities for children to reread their books over the next few days.

Science connections

In this activity children will create models of fossil specimens.

Materials: small plastic freezer trays (from frozen dinners), dinosaur models, chicken bones (from which all the meat has been removed), modeling clay

Preparation: Have children bring in the following items from home: freezer trays, dinosaur models (labeled with the owner's name), chicken bones.

- Have children recall the animals they met in *Animals From Long Ago.* Have them name an animal from long ago and the animal from today that it is related to. Tell children that paleontologists, or people who study animals from long ago, learn about ancient animals by studying their bones and their footprints that have been left in rock. These ancient bones and footprints are called fossils. Tell children that they are going to make their own fossils.
- Distribute a freezer tray and modeling clay to each child or pair of children. Have children fill the trays with clay. Tell children they can either make fossils of dinosaur footprints (called trackways) or dinosaur bones. For the footprints, have children use the feet of dinosaur models to make the foot impressions in the clay. Children might want to experiment by showing several different kinds of dinosaur prints close together or by making footprints that show a herbivore being pursued by a carnivore. For fossil bones, have children arrange the chicken bones in the clay and press down.

- Call on children to display their fossils and to describe the animal from long ago that the fossil represents. Provide assistance as needed. Have them write captions for their fossils and make a display.

Reading and writing science

- Collect books on dinosaurs, other extinct animals, and modern-day animals. Have children bring in their own books from home. Children should work with a partner to look for other present-day animals that resemble animals of long ago. Each pair can present their findings to the group, experimenting with different ways of presenting their information, including labels or a sentence as part of their presentation.

Cross-curricular activity/math

- Cut out two large footprints of an Apatosaur (dinosaur) from a large sheet of chart paper. Each footprint should be a rectangular shape about 1 1/2 feet wide and 3 feet long, with five toes at the end. Display the two footprints to children, and have them estimate how many of their feet would fill the two dinosaur footprints. Write their estimates on the chalkboard. Then provide children with chart paper. Have each child place a foot on the paper, trace the outline, and cut it out. Have children take turns pasting their footprints on the dinosaur footprint. Be sure that children paste the footprints as close to each other as possible. When all the footprints have been pasted down, have children count the number of footprints on the dinosaur feet and compare with the estimates on the chalkboard.

Home/school connections

- Encourage children to work with their families to make a list of present-day animals that face extinction and the possible reasons why.
- Invite children to take the mini-book home to share with their families.

Non-fiction:

- Aliki. *Fossils Tell of Long Ago*. Rev. ed. New York: HarperCollins, 1990.
- Aliki. *Wild and Wooly Mammoths*. New York: HarperCollins, 1996.
- Berger, Melvin. *The World of Dinosaurs*. New York: Newbridge Educational Publishing, 1994.
- Davis, Lee. *Dinosaur Dinners*. New York: DK Publishing, 1998.
- Most, Bernard. *How Big Were the Dinosaurs?* San Diego: Harcourt, 1994.

Fiction:

- Hoff, Syd. *Danny and the Dinosaur*. New York: HarperCollins, 1993.
- Martin, Rafe. *Will's Mammoth*. Illustrated by Stephen Gammell. New York: Putnam, 1989.
- Osborne, Mary Pope. *Sunset of the Sabertooth*. Illustrated by Sal Murdocca. New York: Random House, 1996.

Animal Messengers

Standards
Characteristics of organisms

Benchmarks
Information can be sent and received in many different ways.

Supports
- consistent text patterns
- clear text/photo layout

Challenges
- index
- diagram
- dialogue

Text features
Punctuation: dialogue marks

High-frequency words: *have, send, talk, write*

Blends: *fl, pr*

Suffixes: *s* and *es*

Vowels: *ou* in *sound, out, touch*

Introducing the text

- Tell children the name of the book. Discuss the front- and back-cover photographs. What messages are these animal messengers sending? How are they sending the messages?
- Draw on children's prior knowledge to discuss other ways animals send messages. End the discussion by comparing this with the ways people send messages.

The first reading

Title page: Read the title together. Look at the photo and briefly discuss dolphins.

Pages 2–5: Have children survey the photographs and find those that match their introductory discussion. Encourage them to check print details to confirm their predictions.

Pages 6–7: Model the language on page 6. Discuss how the snake sends its message. Ask what the sound means and have children work out the words written

People have many ways to send messages.

	as dialogue. Read the last line of print together.
Pages 8-15:	Continue to survey the photographs and text. Draw children's attention to the structure of the text and model new and challenging words and sentence structures through discussion. Encourage children to monitor their prediction by checking letter/sound information and meaning.

My cat is telling me something.

Page 16: Model how to use the index.

Have the children read the book independently. Observe their reading behaviors and strategies. Are they recognizing and using the text structure? Using meaning to make predictions? Using effective strategies to learn unfamiliar words?

Rereading and discussing
- Invite responses to the book. What pages did children particularly enjoy? What questions do they have? How could they research their questions?
- Comment on the use of effective strategies you observed and focus briefly on a relevant teaching point. Then have children use the index to choose two parts of their book to reread to a buddy.

Science connections
In this activity children will observe how ants in an ant community communicate.

Materials: cheese, bread, small amount of honey

Preparation: Before conducting this activity, locate some anthills near your school. Place a small saucer of honey or sugar water near each one. During the field trip, children can observe the trail the ants have made to the food.

Note: Some ants, such as fire ants, can inflict a painful bite. Caution children to stay some distance from these ants. When observing, remind children not to step on the anthills or disturb the routine of the colony.

- Have children recall some of the animals they met in *Animal Messengers*. Ask them to describe some of the ways these animals communicate. Review with them that some animals communicate by calls, songs, barks, and squeaks. Others communicate by scent, touch, and by physical signals that animals recognize. For example, a dog wags its tail when it is happy. A cat swishes its tail before it pounces on a mouse. Tell children that they are going to watch a community of ants to learn how they communicate.
- Have children observe the ants as they move along the trail they have made to the food. Have children note the antennae on the ants' heads. Point out that the ant uses the antennae to touch and

feel the food and to communicate with other ants. Place an obstacle on one of the paths. Have children observe how the ants get around the obstacle.
- Place small bits of cheese or bread near one of the trails. Watch what happens. About how long does it take for one ant to find the food? How does the first ant tell the other ants about the food?
- After the field trip, call on children to share what they learned about the way ants communicate.

Reading and writing science

- Ask children to think about what they saw on their field trip. Have them draw a picture illustrating one of the things they noticed. Have them write a sentence under the drawing. Give children time to display their drawings to the rest of the class and to read their sentences aloud.

Cross-curricular activity/social studies

- Tell children that people use speech to communicate with other people and they also use gestures to communicate. Smile and ask children what the smile communicates (happiness). Put your hands on your hips and frown and ask what that gesture communicates (displeasure). Call on volunteers to display other gestures. Have the class tell what each gesture means. You may suggest that children think of gestures that would communicate the following words: *stop, go, come, hi, good-bye, unhappiness, fear, anger, puzzlement, excitement.*

Home/school connections

- Encourage children to observe and record, over several days, how they and their families send messages to each other. At the same time, ask them to record any ways they see or hear animals sending messages. Share these with the group. Explore different ways to categorize the information.
- Invite children to take the mini-book home to share with their families.

Non-fiction:

- Arnosky, Jim. *All about Rattlesnakes*. New York: Scholastic, 1997.
- Cole, Joanna. *The Magic School Bus Inside a Beehive*. Illustrated by Bruce Degen. New York: Scholastic, 1996.
- Demuth, Patricia. *Gorillas*. Illustrated by Pam Lopez. New York: Grossett & Dunlap, 1994.
- McNultey, Faith. *Listening to Whales Sing*. New York: Scholastic, 1994.
- Singer, Marilyn. *Prairie Dogs Kiss and Lobsters Wave: How Animals Say Hello*. Illustrated by Normand Chartier. New York: Henry Holt, 1998.

Fiction:

- Conrad, Pam. *The Rooster's Gift*. Illustrated by Eric Beddoes. New York: HarperCollins, 1996.
- Graff, Nancy Price. *In the Hush of the Evening*. Illustrated by G. Brian Karas. New York: HarperCollins, 1998.
- Polacco, Patricia. *Just Plain Fancy*. New York: Dell, 1994.

At the Playground   A

Standards
Position and motion of objects

Benchmarks
Things move in different ways, such as straight, zigzag, round and round, back and forth, fast and slow. The way to change how something is moving is to give it a push or a pull.

Supports
- consistent layout
- some repetitive language

Challenges
- variety of sentence structures

Text features
High-frequency words: *come, will, have, down, up, fun, around, other*

Blends: *fl, pl, sc, sl, sp, sw*

Compound word: *playground*

Introducing the text
- Tell children the book describes what some children do at the playground. Challenge them to find the word *playground*, then to read the title.
- Encourage children to discuss what they do on the playground. How do they use the structures and games there? How do they use their bodies to climb, push, swing, and so on? Develop the concept of the relationship between force and motion.

The first reading

Title page: Read the title together. Practice chunking the word *playground*.

Pages 2-3: Ask *What is the girl telling you?* Have children silently read these pages before sharing the information.

Pages 4-9: Briefly survey the photographs and print to establish the structure of the text. Demonstrate how to cross-check using clues from photographs, meaning, text structure, and letter/sound relationships.

I slide down, down, down.

Pages 10-13: Ask: *How does the girl use her legs to go back and forth?* Continue to pose questions and have children read silently to find the answers.

Pages 14-16: Ask children to skim these pages and to raise any questions they have.

When you are satisfied the children have a framework for success, ask them to return to the cover and read independently. Observe children's behaviors and strategies as they read their books. Are they using the structure of the text to maintain meaning? Are they cross-checking print and photographs? Using letter/sound knowledge effectively?

Rereading and discussing

- Invite responses. What would they like to know more about? What did they learn? Comment on effective strategies you observe. Ask children to reread their books independently. Over the next few days provide opportunities for them to read their books again.

Science connections

In this activity children will explore how things move and the way to change how something is moving.

- Ask children to recall what they read in *At the Playground*. Have them describe the things they read about and the ways they moved. Write their responses on the chalkboard. Elicit from them that to change the way something is moving is to give it a push or a pull. Demonstrate with the door to the classroom. Begin to shut the door and then pull back on the knob. Have children draw the conclusion that movement of the door changed when you pulled back on the knob. Tell children they will have the opportunity to explore the ways things move by visiting a playground.
- Take children to the school or neighborhood playground. Tell children you are going to give them some time to play at the playground, but as they play on the various equipment, they are to think about the different ways they are moving. As children play, move among them and ask: *How are you moving? Are you moving slowly or fast? How could you change the way you are moving?*
- Back in the classroom, discuss the playground activities. Ask children in what ways they moved, and what they did to change direction. Write children's responses on the chalkboard.

Reading and writing science

- Have children draw pictures of their favorite playground activity, using their books as references. Call on them to write three sentences that describe the way they moved during the activity. Have children display their pictures and read their sentences to the class.

- Create a bulletin board entitled, *The Way Things Move*. With the group's help, write the words: *straight, zigzag, round and round, back and forth,* and *fast and slow* on strips of paper and add them to the display. Call on children to find pictures of items that move in these ways and display them under the proper heading. Every few days review the new items that have been added to the bulletin-board display

Cross-curricular activity/language arts

- Ask children to share what they like about their neighborhood playground. Ask them to think about what could be done to the playground to make it even better. As they offer suggestions, write their responses on the chalkboard. When they are finished, review their responses. Tell children they may be able to improve their playground by writing a letter to a city or town official. Discuss with children what they might say in their letter. Help children formulate sentences and write them on the chalkboard. Discuss how the sentences might be ordered. Write the letter to the city or town official using the sentences the class drafted. Call on children to draw pictures to illustrate either the current problems in the park or how the park might look with the new equipment the class is suggesting. Send the letter. Read any response you receive and post it on the bulletin board.

Home/school connections

- Encourage children and their families to make a list of the things in their homes that move. Next to each item they might write the way that object moves: straight, zigzag, back and forth, round and round, or fast and slow. Have children share their lists with the rest of the class.
- Invite children to take the mini-book home to share with their families

Non-fiction:

- Berger, Melvin. *The Human Body*. New York: Newbridge Educational Publishing, 1997.
- Everitt Betsy. *Up the Ladder, Down the Slide*. San Diego: Harcourt, 1998.
- Gibbons, Gail. *Playgrounds*. New York: Holiday House, 1985.
- Morris, Ann. *Play*. Photographs by Ken Heyman. New York: Lothrop, Lee & Shepard, 1998.
- Murphy, Stuart J. *The Greatest Gymnast of All*. Illustrated by Cynthia Jabar. New York: HarperCollins, 1998.

Fiction:

- Aruego, Jose. *Look What I Can Do*. New York: Aladdin, 1988.
- Cole, Joanna. *Norma Jean, Jumping Bean.* Illustrated by Lynn Munsinger. New York: Random House, 1987.
- Havill, Juanita. *Jamaica Tag-Along* Illustrated by Anne Sibly O'Brien. Boston: Houghton Mifflin, 1989.
- Naylor, Phyllis Reynolds. *King of the Playground*. Illustrated by Nola Langer Malone. New York: Atheneum, 1991.

Beaks

Standards
Knows about the diversity and unity that characterize life

Benchmarks
Animals eat and use other plants and animals.

Supports
- repetitive language and sentence structure
- consistent print placement
- strong photo/text match

Challenges
- specialized vocabulary: *toucans, flamingos*

Text features
Punctuation: comma, apostrophe

High-frequency words: *this, have, get, eat, use, they, their*

Compound words: *hummingbird, kingfisher*

Digraphs: *ch, sh, th*

Introducing the text
- Distribute a book to each child and ask them to look at the cover photograph and predict the name of the book. Have them check the beginning and ending letters closely to confirm *Beaks*. Brainstorm what they know about beaks, focusing the talk on descriptions of the beaks and how the different birds use them.

The first reading

Title page: Read the page together and discuss the photograph.

Pages 2-3: Look at the photographs. Model *Birds have beaks.* Ask children to look at page 3 to find out what this bird's beak helps it do.

Pages 4-5: Focus discussion on the name of the bird, the kind of beak it has, and what it is used for. Ask children to locate and read some of these words.

Pages 6-15: Continue to discuss photographs and print. Through conversation, establish the pattern of the text, identify unknown words and

A bird's beak helps it get food and eat it.

3

strategies for working them out, and give children the opportunity to practice what they already know.

Page 16: Have children work this page out. Prompt and support skill and strategy use.

How is this bird using its beak?

Have all children read their books aloud but independently of each other. Observe their skill and strategy use. Are they using print and photographs in an integrated way? Using parts of words to work out new words? Noticing and using punctuation?

Rereading and discussing

- When all children have successfully read the text, invite discussion. What was the most interesting thing they learned about beaks? What questions do they have about the book? What would they like to research? Did some students find parts of the text challenging? How did they go about solving challenges? Look at one of the compound words and discuss ways to work it out. Ask the children to find the other one. Have children reread their books.

Science connections

In this activity children will observe birds eating and will draw conclusions about how beaks function.

Materials: wild birdseed or bread crumbs

- Call on children to name the birds they met in *Beaks*. Have them describe the beak each bird has and the food it eats. Point out to children that the toucan has a beak that is good for eating fruit. The parrot has a beak that is good for cracking open seeds and nuts. Tell them they are going to observe how birds use their beaks for eating.
- Go to the school playground or neighborhood park with children. Throw out birdseed or bread crumbs to attract birds. Have children observe the birds as they eat. Help them identify the different birds feeding and the shape of each beak.
- Back in the classroom, have children draw pictures of the birds they saw. Have them write one sentence describing the bird's beak on the bottom of their drawings.

Reading and writing science

- Have children look through nature magazines or calendars to find and cut out pictures of birds. Explain to children that by looking at beaks they can pretty much figure out what a bird eats. Explain that insect eaters have sharp, pointed beaks (warbler); fish eaters have long, sharp, pointed beaks (heron); grass eaters have short, rounded beaks (ostrich); birds with ducklike beaks use them to strain water for food; birds who hunt have beaks with a sharp

hook on the end. Have children display their bird pictures and describe each bird's beak. Have children paste their bird pictures in a row at the top of a piece of poster paper. Underneath each picture, have children write what that bird eats.
- Challenge children to draw a picture of an imaginary bird with an incredible beak. Tell them the beak should give a good idea of what the bird eats. For example, a bird with a soupspoon for a beak would eat soup and could be called a "soup sipper." Have children draw their birds and write down the bird's name. They then can present their birds to the class, and describe the beaks and the food the birds eat.

Cross-curricular activity/social studies
- Tell children that each fall millions of birds fly from North America to the rain forests of Central and South America. They return again each spring to build nests and raise their young. Have children recount any of the experiences they might have had seeing birds fly south. Using a large map of North and South America, trace the migration route from your town to Central or South America. Help children calculate the distance. Tell children that some birds are able to fly the long distance in only three to five days.

Home/school connections
- Encourage children and their families to look for birds in their neighborhood and to describe each bird's beak. If possible, children and their families could draw pictures of the birds and write their names. Other information can also be added, such as the kind of food each bird eats.
- Invite children to take the mini-book home to share with their families.

Non-fiction:
- Arnosky, Jim. *Crinkleroot's 25 Birds Every Child Should Know*. New York: Simon & Schuster, 1993.
- McMillan, Bruce. *Puffins Climb, Penguins Rhyme*. San Diego: Harcourt, 1995.
- Oppenheim, Joanne. *Have You Seen Birds?* Illustrated by Barbara Reid. New York: Scholastic, 1989.
- Wood, Audrey. *Birdsong*. Illustrated by Robert Florczak. San Diego: Harcourt, 1997.

Fiction:
- Johnston, Tony. *The Old Woman and the Birds*. Illustrated by Stephanie Garcia. San Diego: Harcourt, 1994.
- Keller, Holly. *Island Baby*. New York: Morrow, 1993.
- Sun, Chyng Feng. *Square Beak*. Boston: Houghton Mifflin, 1993.

Bikes
A

Standards
Abilities of technological design

Benchmarks
Most things are made of parts.

Something may not work if some of its parts are missing.

Supports
- familiar topic
- descriptive language

Challenges
- specialized language
- labeled diagram

Text features
Punctuation: exclamation point

High-frequency words: *there, ride, people, have, hold, around, if, then, name*

Blends: *fl, st, tr*

Digraphs: *ch, th, wh*

Introducing the text
- Discuss the front- and back-cover photographs and read the title together.
- Draw on children's prior experiences with bicycles to discuss what parts most bikes have, the use of each part, and what happens if a part breaks.

The first reading

Title page: Invite children to read the title and talk about the photograph.

Pages 2–3: Briefly survey the photographs. Model the introductory sentence. Point out that this kind of introduction is often used in a non-fiction book.

Pages 4–12: Continue to support discussion as children browse through the photographs and text. Prompt children to recognize and use the layout and text pattern that introduces a bike part on a left-hand page and tells about it on the facing page. Model ways they can use their knowledge about bikes to predict the text.

This bike has two big wheels and two little training wheels.

Page 13: Ask what is happening here.

Pages 14-15: Ask how the boy is solving his problem.

Page 16: Model how to use the arrowed labels. Invite children to use these to find and read some of the parts.

Flat tires can be fixed.
The boy pumps air into the tire.

When you are confident that the children have enough information to read the book independently, have children read their books as you observe their behaviors and strategies. Are they cross-checking text and photographs? Monitoring meaning? Self-correcting soon after a miscue?

Rereading and discussing

- Invite responses to the book. Ask which parts individuals found most challenging. Discuss strategies for reading one or two of these parts. Discuss how their own knowledge and experience with bikes helped them to read this book.
- Have children read their books independently to themselves or a friend.

Science connections

In this activity children will observe how a bicycle works.

Materials: a two-wheeled bike with training wheels

Preparation: Arrange for a parent to bring in a child's bicycle. It is best to conduct this activity in the gymnasium or at a playground.

- Ask children to describe some of their experiences riding bikes. Ask them to recall what things they learned when they read *Bikes* and what new information surprised them. Write their responses on chart paper. Tell children that they will examine a bike and learn more about its parts.
- Display the bicycle in an open area. Call on volunteers to name the parts they know and to describe the function of each part. For example, the handlebars let you steer the bike. The brakes let you stop the bike. Point out other features of the bike, if children do not name them. Be sure to show children the wheel gear and the chain that runs from the pedal to the back wheel. Demonstrate how moving the pedal moves the chain and the back wheel.
- Ask children what would happen if one of the parts of the bike broke. Help children see that if a part broke, the bike would not work properly.

Reading and writing science

- Draw or cut out pictures of several toys with missing parts, such as a skateboard with a missing wheel, a wagon with no handle, a kite with no string, a model train with a section of track missing. Call on children to name and draw the missing part. Then help them to label the important parts of each toy.

- Have children write bike riddles to try to stump their classmates. Provide each child with a large index card. Ask each child to think of one part of a bicycle. Have them write the name of that part on one side of the index card. On the other side, have them write three simple clues about the part. Model some sample clues for children and write them on a chart so that children can refer to them. Call on children to read their clues to the group. Have the group guess what bike part is being described. Keep the chart on your wall for children to use as a reference for other writing experiences

Cross-curricular activity/health and safety

- Have children talk about their experiences riding bicycles. Tell them that bike riding is fun, but it is important to follow safety rules to make sure they don't get hurt when they ride their bikes. Ask each child to name some safety rules that they follow when they ride their bikes. Write the rules on chart paper, elaborating on them if necessary and adding some if children do not mention them. When you are finished, review the rules with children. Ask each child to choose one rule to illustrate. Provide construction paper and drawing materials. Have children write the rule at the top of their papers and then illustrate it. Hang the completed drawings in the school corridor.

Home/school connections

- Working with their families, have children draw and label parts of an item in their home, such as a lamp, a door, or a chair.
- Invite children to take the mini-book home to share with their families

Non-fiction:

- Berger, Melvin. *Simple Machines.* New York: Newbridge Educational Publishing, 1995.
- Crews Donald *Bicycle Race.* New York: Greenwillow, 1985.
- Gibbons, Gail. *The Bicycle Book.* New York: Holiday House, 1995.
- Rockwell, Anne. *Bikes.* New York: Dutton, 1991.

Fiction:

- Ball, Duncan. *Grandfather's Wheelything.* Illustrated by Cat Bowman Smith. New York: Simon & Schuster, 1994.
- Berenstain, Stan and Janice. *Bike Lesson.* New York: Random House, 1966.
- Harder, Dan. *Colliding with Chris.* Illustrated by Kevin O'Malley. New York: Hyperion, 1998.
- Heine, Helme. *Friends.* New York: Aladdin, 1986.
- Pilkey, Dav. *The Paperboy.* New York: Orchard, 1996.

City Buildings

Standards
Understands basic concepts about the structure and properties of matter

Benchmarks
Objects can be described in terms of the materials they are made of and their physical properties—color, size, shape.

Supports
- strong photo/text match
- some repetitive language and sentence structure

Challenges
- variety of sentence structures
- specialized vocabulary: *metal, concrete, brownstone*

Text features
Punctuation: period

High-frequency words: *take, look, many, come, this, small, wide, long, thin, round, work, called*

Blends: *sc, scr, sk, sm*

Digraphs: *ph, sh, th, wh*

Compound word: *brownstone*

Introducing the text
- Give each child a book. Invite discussion about the front and back covers. Where would they see buildings like these? Can they see a word in the title that could be *city*? Read the title together and draw on children's prior knowledge to discuss sizes, shapes, and materials found in city buildings and in their own homes.

The first reading

Title page: Read the title page together. Discuss the shapes and sizes of the buildings in the photograph.

Page 2: Model the first line and ask: *What will you see?* Have children find and read: *You will see many buildings.*

Page 3: Ask: *What can you see that is different about these city buildings?* Discuss the different sizes.

Pages 4–5: Discuss what is different about the buildings here. Model language structure and content.

City buildings come in different sizes.

3

Pages 6-9: Continue discussing photos and modeling some of the language. Ask children to use letter-sound knowledge and meaning to confirm some predictions.

Page 10: Model *City buildings can be made out of different things.* Ask: *What is this building made mostly of?* Have children read the answer.

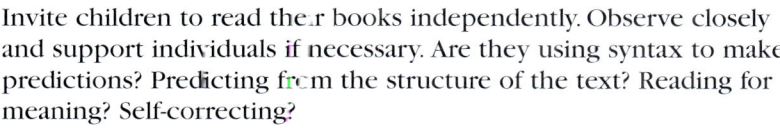
These buildings are made mostly of wood.

Pages 11-13: Have children check what each building is made mostly of.

Pages 14-16: Focus discussion on kinds of buildings and what they are used for.

Invite children to read their books independently. Observe closely and support individuals if necessary. Are they using syntax to make predictions? Predicting from the structure of the text? Reading for meaning? Self-correcting?

Rereading and discussing

- Discuss which buildings they liked and why. Comment on effective reading strategies you observed.
- Ask children to look through the book to identify blends.
- Ask children to read their books again, independently or with a buddy.

Science connections

In this activity children will identify and describe the physical properties of buildings in their neighborhood.

- Have children recall some of the buildings they read about in *City Buildings*. Review with them some of the physical properties of these buildings and the materials they were made of. Ask children to name and describe some buildings in their own neighborhood. Prompt them to describe the shape and size of the building, the color, the number of windows it has, and the materials it is made of. Then tell children they are going to take a walk in their own neighborhood to see these and other buildings.
- Walk through the neighborhood with children, stopping to point out various buildings to them. Encourage children to describe the physical properties of the buildings. Help them identify parts of the buildings that are different shapes.
- Back in the classroom, have each child draw a picture of their favorite building. Have children write one sentence describing a physical property of the building at the bottom of their drawings.

Reading and writing science

- With children, brainstorm to come up with words that describe buildings. Have children think about the shape of buildings, the

size, color, and the materials they are made of. Create a bulletin-board display titled, "Words That Tell About Buildings." Encourage children to suggest descriptive words. Write the words children suggest on strips of paper and add them to the display. Continue adding new words daily. Every few days, review the new words that have been posted.
- Have children work in pairs to write about buildings. Provide each pair with a picture of a building or have them look through magazines to find one they like. On a separate sheet of paper have them write three sentences that describe their building. You may want to write some model sentences on the chalkboard for children to use, such as: *This building is (big, small, wide, tall). This building has (many, few) windows. This building is made mostly of (wood, metal, cement, brick, steel).*
- When they are done, have partners read what they have written to the rest of the class.

Cross-curricular activity/social studies
- Have children create their own city buildings, using boxes and cans. Have each child bring in an empty box or can from home. Provide children with large sheets of construction paper. Have them cover the boxes or cans with the paper and then, using crayons or markers, create the windows, doors, and any ornamentation. Have each child present the completed building to the rest of the class. The child should describe the building and tell what it is used for (library, store, home, office building, and so on). After the presentations, have children create several city blocks with their buildings.

Home/school connections
- Encourage children and their families to identify and describe the shape, color, and size of their own homes, as well as the materials they are made out of.
- Invite children to take the mini-book home to share with their families.

Non-fiction:
- Barton, Byron. *Machines at Work.* New York: HarperCollins, 1987.
- Florian, Douglas. *City Streets.* New York: Greenwillow, 1990.
- Gibbons, Gail. *Up Goes the Skyscraper!* New York: Atheneum, 1990.
- Wellington, Monica. *Night City.* New York: Dutton, 1998.

Fiction and poetry:
- Burton, Virginia Lee. *Mike Mulligan and His Steam Shovel.* Boston: Houghton Mifflin, 1967.
- Derby, Sally. *My Steps.* Illustrated by Adjoa Burrowes. New York: Lee & Low, 1996.
- Merriam, Eve. *Bam Bam Bam.* Illustrated by Dan Yaccarino. New York: Henry Holt, 1996.
- Patrick, Denise Lewis. *The Car Washing Street.* Illustrated by John Ward. New York: Tambourine/Greenwillow, 1993.
- Waber, Bernard. *The House on East Eighty-Eighth Street.* Boston: Houghton Mifflin, 1962.

Day and Night A

Standards
Understands basic features of earth

Benchmarks
The sun can be seen only during the day, but the moon can be seen sometimes at night, and sometimes during the day. The sun, moon, and stars all appear to move slowly across the sky.

Supports
- consistent layout
- moderate photo/text match

Challenges
- specialized vocabulary
- variety of sentence structures

Text features
High-frequency words: *you, out, morning, now, can, when, but, time, over*

Blends: *sk, st*

Digraphs: *th, wh*

Introducing the text

- Read the title and draw on children's experiences to talk about what can be seen in the sky during the day and what can be seen at night. Focus discussion on the way the sun and moon appear to move slowly across the sky, and how the moon's appearance changes during each month.

The first reading

Title page: Read together.

Pages 2-7: Talk briefly about the photographs and text. Model the text structure by asking: *What is this photograph helping you know about the sun? What time of day is it? Where is the sun now?* Have children check print and photographs to confirm their replies.

Pages 8-12: Continue building a framework for children's independent reading. Encourage them to cross-check the written information with the clues in the photographs and to recognize the sequential structure of the text.

Now the sun is high in the sky.

Pages 13-16: Continue to build a framework for children's independent reading by prompting them to think about print and photo cues in an integrated way and to check their predictions constantly by asking: *Does it sound right? Does it look right? Does it make sense?*

Finally, it is a full moon.

When you are satisfied that they have sufficient information to successfully read the book independently, ask children to read their books on their own. Observe their strategies and behaviors. Are they cross-checking photographs and text? Self-correcting after a miscue? Using phrasing? Give support when necessary to help individuals problem-solve independently.

Rereading and discussing

- Share responses to the book. Have children ever done any of these activities? Did they do them the same way or differently? What did they find out? Ask if anyone wants to tell about a good strategy he or she used, and make a teaching point from the strategy.
- Ask children to read their book to themselves or a buddy.

Science connections

In this activity children will explore why the sun and the moon appear to move across the sky.

Materials: a large light-colored balloon, two flashlights, a felt-tipped marker

Preparation: Blow up the balloon, and use the marker to draw some small houses, trees, and stick figures in the middle of one small area.

- Ask children to recall what they read in *Day and Night*. Ask children to tell you what the position of the sun is in the early morning, afternoon, and late afternoon. Ask children if they think the sun moves across the sky. Write their responses on the chalkboard. Tell them that they will do an experiment to understand why the sun appears to move across the sky.
- Display the balloon and tell children to imagine that the figures and houses represent the town where they live. Ask two volunteers to be the sun and the moon. Provide each with a flashlight. Have the "sun" stand to your left and the "moon" stand to your right. Ask each to turn on their flashlights. Explain to children that the earth rotates, making one complete turn every 24 hours. Have children note where on the balloon the sun is shining. Slowly rotate the balloon toward the sun. Have children note where the sun is shining now. Continue rotating the balloon until the sun is no longer shining on

the town. Ask children to note what is shining on the town now (the moon). Continue to rotate the balloon slowly, and ask children to note where the moon is shining on the balloon as you move it.
- Help children draw conclusions based on their experiment. Call on volunteers to describe the experiment in their own words.

Reading and writing science

- Create a word web for night and day. Ask children to think of words that describe night or objects that they would see at night, such as the moon or stars. Write their responses on the chalkboard. Do the same for day. Tell children they are going to use the words to create poems. Write the word *Night* at the top of a piece of chart paper. Ask children to read the words for night from the word web. Write them on the chart paper, ending with the word *night*. Do the same with day. Read the poems aloud to children. Invite volunteers to read them aloud to the class.

Cross-curricular activity/art

Materials: drawing paper, crayons

- Tell the children they are going to make "day" and "night" pictures. Ask children to choose a place in the neighborhood and to draw two pictures of it. Tell them to try to make the pictures identical, but one should show what happens during the day and one should show what happens during the night. Tell children to completely color in all shapes in the pictures, not just outline them. Have children label one picture "day" and the other "night." When the pictures are complete, display them.

Home/school connections

- Encourage children and their families to talk about something they enjoy doing together during the day and something they enjoy doing together during the evening. Have children list each activity and share their lists with the class.
- Invite children to take the mini-book home to share with their families.

Non-fiction:

- Bendick, Jeanne. *Sun*. Brookfield, CT: Millbrook Press, 1991.
- Branley, Franklyn. *What Makes Day and Night?* Illustrated by Arthur Dorros. New York: HarperTrophy, 1994.
- Gibbons, Gail. *Sun Up, Sun Down*. San Diego: Harcourt, 1983.
- Trumbauer Lisa. *What Is a Cycle?* New York: Newbridge Educational Publishing, 1998.

Fiction:

- Ackerman, Karen. *By the Dawn's Early Light*. Illustrated by Catherine Stock. New York: Simon & Schuster, 1994.
- Asch, Frank. *Moondance*. New York: Scholastic, 1993.
- Gollub, Matthew. *The Moon Was at a Fiesta*. New York: Morrow, 1994.
- McDermott, Gerald. *Musicians of the Sun: An Aztec Myth*. New York: Simon & Schuster, 1997.
- Pfister, Maurice. *Sun and Moon*. New York: Scholastic, 1993.

How Animals Move

Standards
Knows about the diversity and unity that characterize life

Benchmarks
Some animals and plants are alike in the way they look and in the things they do and others are very different from one another.

Supports
- moderate to strong photo/text match
- repetitive language

Challenges
- specialized vocabulary: *manatee*
- continuous print across three pages

Text features
Punctuation: comma, ellipses

High-frequency words: *this, can, the, in, help, fast, swim*

Blends: *cl, fl, fr, st, sw*

Introducing the text
- Explain to children that the book is about how animals move.
- Locate these words in the title and read them together.
- Discuss different ways the children can move.
- Brainstorm ways animals move. Focus the discussion by asking: *What animals can hop? Swim? Run?*

The first reading

Title page: Read the title page together. Confirm that this is the same print as on the cover.

Pages 2-3: Survey the photograph and ask: *Who can fly? What helps the bee fly in and out of flowers? What helps the bird fly across the sea?*
Model how to check print and photographs to see if predictions make sense.

Pages 4-5: Continue to model the language structure and content in a conversational way.

Pages 6-7: Ask what children can see in the photos that helps a kangaroo and a frog hop. Help the

This bee can fly.
Little wings help the bee fly in and out of flowers.

	children use effective strategies to work out "strong back legs."
Pages 8–9:	What's the *frog* using its strong back legs to do here? Notice the silent b in *climb*.
Pages 10–11:	What else can swim? Help children chunk the word *manatee* to work it out.
Pages 12–14:	Model *Animals move in so many ways*. Ask where the animals are in each photograph. Have children check the print to confirm predictions.
Page 15:	Ask: *Who is moving now? Yes, people move in different ways.*
Page 16:	Challenge children to work out this page.

Animals move in so many ways. They move in the water...

Observe closely as each child reads his/her book aloud independently.

- Can they use the repetitive sentence structure to maintain momentum? Are they confidently reading some high-frequency words? Are they monitoring meaning? Do they use a variety of strategies to work out unknown words?
- Prompt and praise children to help keep them reading independently.

Rereading and discussing

- When all of the children have finished, discuss what interested them the most and what they would like to know more about. Comment positively on successful strategies and observed behaviors.
- Discuss ellipsis points and reread pages 7–9.
- Discuss tricky words individual children encountered and ways to work them out.
- Ask children to read their books independently or with a buddy.

Science connections

In this activity children will identify the ways different animals move and the body parts that help in locomotion.

- Remind children that in *How Animals Move* they learned about the different ways animals move and the body parts that help them move that way. Call upon volunteers to name one of the animals and demonstrate how that animal moved. Have children say what body parts the animal used. Then ask children to name other animals that move that way.
- Take a trip to a nearby park or to a pet shop to observe animals. As children view each animal, help them decide how the animal moves and what body parts it uses to move. Back in the classroom, call on children to name the animals they saw, the ways

they move, and the body parts used in locomotion. Record children's responses in table form on a large chart.

Reading and writing science

- Have children create their own "books" about how animals move. Have each child draw a picture of a favorite animal in motion. Write these sentences on the board:

    This (animal)   can (movement)   .

    (Body parts)   help the (animal)   (movement)   .

- Have children use some of the sentence patterns from *How Animals Move,* using the book as a reference. Have them write the sentences at the bottom of their pictures, filling in the appropriate information in the blanks. Have groups make a cover for their book and staple the pages together. The groups can then share their books by reading them aloud to the rest of the group.

Cross-curricular activity/movement exploration

- Find a piece of classical music with a variety of rhythms and moods for children to listen and move to as if they were different animals. After the activity allow children time to share what animals they became, how they moved, and which "body parts" they used to move in that way.

Home/school connections

- Suggest that children and their families keep a record of the animals they see around them and the ways they move. Keep a chart in the classroom where children can add a check mark when they observe those animals listed. After a week have children tally the number of check marks for each animal.
- Invite children to take the mini-book home to share with their families.

Non-fiction:

- Berger, Melvin. *Leaping Frogs*. New York: Newbridge Educational Publishing, 1996.
- Jenkins, Steve. *Biggest, Strongest, Fastest*. Boston: Ticknor & Fields, 1994.
- McNulty, Faith. *Dancing with Manatees*. Illustrated by Lena Shiffman. New York: Scholastic, 1994.
- Morrison, Taylor. *Cheetah*. New York: Henry Holt, 1998.

Fiction:

- Carle, Eric. *From Head to Toe*. New York: HarperCollins, 1997.
- Ginsburg, Mirra. *The Chick and the Duckling.* Illustrated by Jose Aruego and Ariane Dewey. New York: Aladdin, 1988.
- Mora, Pat. *The Race of Toad and Deer*. New York: Greenwillow, 1995.
- Walsh, Ellen Stoll. *Hop Jump*. San Diego: Harcourt. 1993.

Kittens   A

Standards
Characteristics of organisms

Benchmarks
Things can change in different ways such as size, color, weight, movement. Some small changes can be detected by taking measurements.

Supports
- moderate photo/text match
- headings

Challenges
- contents page
- scale diagram

Text features
High-frequency words: *and, they, not, can, mother, their, first, by, like*

Blends: *cl, gr, pl, sp*

Compound word: *cannot*

Introducing the text

- Challenge children to read the title. Ask what the cover photograph helps them to know.
- Then draw on their prior knowledge and experiences to talk about kittens. Focus the discussion on what kittens can do and what they look like as they grow and change.

The first reading

Contents page: Show children the contents page, and read it with them. Have them speculate on possible information they will find in each time period.

Pages 2-3: Ask children to look at the photograph and text to find out what they tell about the kittens.

Pages 4-5: Talk about the photographs. Ask: *What can you see here? Can you find those words in the text?*

Pages 6-9: Read the heading together, and discuss how the kittens have grown and changed. Ask children to find and read the words that tell what the mother cat still does for her kittens.

Their eyes are not open.
Their ears are not open.
They cannot walk.

Pages 10-13: Read the heading together. Continue to survey the photographs, and encourage children to check text details to find out how the kittens have grown and changed.

Pages 14-15: Model how the chart gives cumulative information about the weight of the kittens.

Page 16: Have children predict the words, then check print details together to check their predictions.

Observe as children read their books aloud, but independently of others. Are they using headings? Noticing and reading the pronoun changes? Using known words to figure out unfamiliar words, such as *bigger*?

Rereading and discussing

- Invite children's responses to the book. Ask them to compare their own experiences with kittens to the information in the book. Use the book to make a teaching point of the words *them* and *they*.
- Have children turn to the contents page and use it to choose which part of the book they will read to a buddy.
- Provide opportunities for children to reread their books during the next few days.

Science connections

In this activity children will discuss how they have changed since they were babies.

Materials: Have children bring in one of their baby pictures.

- Discuss with children what they learned in *Kittens*. Have them relate the ways that the kittens changed. Display two baby pictures. Ask children to name the children in the pictures. Ask children to describe what the babies look like—their size, color of their hair, amount of hair, color of eyes, number of teeth, etc. Ask children what kind of things babies can do by themselves.
- Have children compare the two baby pictures with the two children in the class who brought them in. Have children describe how they have physically changed since they were babies. Point out any change in hair or eye color. Ask them to name the things the children can do now that they couldn't do when they were babies.
- Give each child an opportunity to display his or her baby picture. Have children briefly describe what they looked like as babies, what they could do, and how they have changed since that time. Display the baby pictures on the bulletin board.

Reading and writing science

- Provide each child with a large sheet of drawing paper (11" x 17"). Demonstrate for children how to fold it so that there are three sections. Tell children you want them to draw a picture of themselves in each section. In the first section, have them draw a picture of themselves when they were babies. In the second section, have them draw a picture of themselves as they are now. In the third section, have them draw a picture of what they imagine they will look like when they are adults. Have children write a sentence about themselves for each drawing. As children share their drawings, discuss with them how they will change in different ways as they get older.

Cross-curricular activity/music/movement exploration

Materials: a cassette player and a tape of classical music

- Conduct this activity in the school gym or other large area. Tell children that you are going to play some music for about 15 minutes and you want them to move to the music. Have each child find a space. Tell them you want them to first imagine that they are tiny babies and to move to the music as a tiny baby might. Play the music and ask children to move like a baby. As the music continues, suggest to children that they are a bit older and can crawl and stand. Then suggest to them that they can walk. Then have children imagine they are young children who can jump, run, skip, dance, and hop. Caution children not to bump into a neighbor as they move to the music. Finally suggest that they move like teenagers. After the music stops, have children share their thoughts about the movement.

Home/school connections

- Encourage adult members of each child's family to share their own baby pictures with the children. Have children and their families talk about how living things change as they mature.
- Invite children to take the mini-book home to share with their families.

Non-fiction:

- Berger, Melvin. *Squirrels All Year Long.* New York: Newbridge Educational Publishing, 1992.
- Bonners, Susan. *Why Does the Cat Do That?* New York: Henry Holt, 1998.
- Cole, Joanna. *My New Kitten.* Illustrated by Margaret Miller. New York: Morrow, 1995.
- Selsam, Millicent E. *How Kittens Grow.* Photographs by Neil Johnson. New York: Scholastic, 1992.

Fiction:

- Asch, Frank. *The Last Puppy.* New York: Aladdin, 1989.
- Fleming, Denise. *Mama Cat Has Three Kittens.* New York: Henry Holt, 1998.
- Newberry, Clare Turlay. *April's Kittens.* New York: Harper, 1993.

Let's Make Something New

Standards
Structure and properties of matter

Benchmarks
Make something out of cardboard, wood, plastic, metal, or existing objects that can be actually used to perform a task.

Supports
- strong photo/text match
- simple procedural text

Challenges
- variety of sentence structures

Text features
Punctuation: apostrophe

High-frequency words: *going, make, new, that, use, those, them, look, push, like, tree, fill*

Compound word: *something*

Introducing the text
- Discuss the front cover. What do the children think this is? What did the father and daughter use to make it? What helps the children to know?
- Draw on children's prior experience to discuss how new things can be made from old things, and why we might want to do this. Bring the discussion to a close by talking about what would be done first and next as the bird feeder is constructed.

The first reading

Title page: Read the title page together. Talk about the items in the photograph and how they might be used to build the bird feeder.

Pages 2-3: Have the children look at the photographs to find out what the girl is throwing out. Ask: *What could her father be saying?* Support children as they work out the text on both pages.

Pages 4-6: Say: *What is it the father tells her not to throw away now?* Read together to confirm. Model the repetitive text again.

Page 7: Ask children to find and read the words

Don't throw out that bottle! We can use it.

	that tell what the father and daughter are going to make.
Pages 8-13:	Model the words that signal the sequence as you talk about these pages. *What is Dad doing first? What does the girl do next? Now what are they doing?*
Pages 14-15:	Ask: *What is happening now?* Briefly discuss the photographs and check some of the language.
Page 16:	Read the page together.

Yes!

Ask the children to turn back to the cover and to quietly read the book aloud, independently of each other. Observe their reading strategies. Are they observing detail in the photographs as they predict? Recognizing and using the sequence that structures the text? Using known words to figure out unfamiliar words? Give prompts if needed to help children maintain and regain meaning.

Rereading and discussing

- Invite discussion about responses to the book. What else could have been used to build a bird feeder?
- Point out the first words that signal the sequence and ask children to find and read the others.
- Ask children to reread *Let's Make Something New* again, either to themselves or with a friend. Make sure they have the opportunity to read the book again independently over the next few days.

Science connections

In this activity children will make bird feeders using plastic bottles, old pens, and twine.

Materials: For each child or group of children you will need: a wide-mouth plastic bottle, two used pens, and about 12 inches of twine. You will also need a ruler and birdseed. Arrange for children to bring these items from home. Before beginning the activity, use a Phillips screwdriver to make two holes about 2 inches from the top on opposite sides of each bottle. Make two holes about 2 inches from the bottom on opposite sides of each bottle.

- Remind children that in *Let's Make Something New*, a young girl and her dad make a bird feeder using recycled materials. Have children name the materials used to make the bird feeder. Then call on children to recount the steps the girl and her father followed to make the feeder. Tell children that they will also have an opportunity to make a bird feeder.
- Distribute the bottles, old pens, and twine to children. Have children thread the twine through the two holes at the top and make a strong knot. Have them push the pens through the holes at the bottom. Lend assistance when necessary. Have children

measure and mark a spot 2 inches above each pen. Using a sharp knife, carefully cut a flap over the spot. (Do not let children handle the knife.) Push the flap in (the flap will prevent birdseed from falling out of the feeder). Have children fill the bird feeder with seed and replace the cap.
- Hang the feeders outside the classroom window or on a nearby tree. (Hang them as high as you can to keep birds safe from predators.) Watch to see which birds come to feed.

Reading and writing science
- Use large sheets of construction paper to create a class nature journal in which children record the birds or animals they see at the bird feeders. Delegate two or three children each day to record what the class observes. These children will draw pictures and write sentences about the birds the class sees at the feeders. (Squirrels and chipmunks might also come.) Use guidebooks to help children identify the birds.

Cross-curricular activity/math
- Create simple word problems using the bird feeder as a theme. For example: *Bob has three plastic bottles. How many old pens will he need to make 3 bird feeders?* (6 pens) *Two birds came to the feeder. Five more birds came. How many birds were at the feeder in all?* (7 birds) Challenge children to make up their own word problems for the class to answer.

Home/school connections
- Encourage children and their families to make something new using recycled items. On a given day, have children bring in their completed objects. Have each child describe what the object is and how it is used. They should also name the recycled items they used to make it and describe the steps they took to create the object.
- Invite children to take the mini-book home to share with their families.

Non-fiction:
- Busch, Phyllis. *Backyard Safaris: 52 Year-Round Science Adventures*. Illustrated by Wayne Trimm. New York: Aladdin, 1995.
- Henley, Judith. *A Piece of String Is a Wonderful Thing*. Cambridge, MA: Candlewick, 1995.
- Rockwell, Anne. *Our Yard Is Full of Birds*. New York: Macmillan, 1992.
- Swineburne, Stephen. *Swallows in the Birdhouse*. Illustrated by Robin Brickman. Brookfield, CT: Millbrook Press, 1996.

Fiction:
- Frank, John. *Odds 'N Ends Alvy*. Illustrated by G. Brian Karas. New York: Simon & Schuster, 1993.
- Keats, Ezra Jack. *Regards to the Man in the Moon*. New York: Atheneum, 1987.
- Neitzel, Shirley. *The House I'll Build for the Wrens*. Illustrated by Nancy Winslow Parker. New York: Greenwillow, 1998.

Rocks   A

Standards
Properties of earth materials

Benchmarks
Chunks of rock come in many sizes and shapes, from boulders to grains of sand and even smaller.

Supports
- strong photo/text match
- repetitive patterns

Challenges
- change in verb tense
- sentence continues across two pages

Text Features
Punctuation: ellipses, exclamation point

High-frequency words: *can, be, there, are, find, come*

Blends: *bl, gr, sm, st*

Digraphs: *sh, th, wh*

Introducing the text

- Discuss the front- and back-cover photographs and ask the children to work out the title.
- Model the language *rocks are everywhere*
- Draw on children's prior knowledge by asking them to tell what they know about rocks. End the discussion by having children brainstorm where rocks can be found.

The first reading

Title page: Invite children to read the title and talk about the photograph.

Pages 2-9:   Ask children to locate the sentence "Rocks are everywhere," then invite them to briefly survey each photograph to find where rocks can be found.

Model the pattern *you can find rocks* and model ways to confirm responses by checking the print.

Pages 10-11:   Say: *Rocks can be many sizes.* Point out that even some grains of sand can be rocks.

You can find rocks in a desert.

Pages 12-15: Ask: *What is different about these rocks?* before discussing the shapes and what they look like, and before reading the print.

Page 16: Ask: *What do the rocks look like?*

Ask the children to turn back to the cover and quietly read the book aloud to themselves, independently of each other. Observe their reading behaviors and strategies. Are they checking photographs and print to predict and confirm? Are they using the text patterns to read with phrasing? Are they noticing the changes from singular to plural? Are they reading for meaning? Give prompts if needed.

Rocks can be many shapes. These rocks look like eggs.

Rereading and discussing

- Invite discussion about responses to the book. What interested children most? What else would they like to find out about rocks? Comment on their strategies for maintaining and regaining meaning. Then ask them to reread *Rocks* to themselves or to a friend. Make sure they have the opportunity to independently read the text again over the next few days.

Science connections

- In this activity children will make comparisons among rocks.
- Have each child bring in a rock or provide a rock for each child. Remind children that rocks are found in many different places. Call on children to name the places where their rocks were found. Encourage children to describe their rocks: Are they smooth or rough? Big or small, round or square, dark or light?
- Then have children work in small groups of five or six. Tell children they are going to compare their rocks. Have children line up the rocks from the smallest to the largest. Then have them line up the rocks from the lightest to the darkest. Have each group decide which rock is the smoothest and which rock is the roughest. Encourage groups to talk about the shape of each rock: Are they round, square, or flat? Have groups share their findings with the class.

Reading and writing science

- Provide children with books about rocks and minerals. Have children look through the books to identify the type of rock they have.
- Invite children to write about their pet rocks. Provide each child with a large index card. Suggest that they give their rocks names. Then have children use simple sentences or phrases to describe their rocks. Have children place their rocks on their desks alongside the index cards. Invite children to visit other desks and read about the rocks on display.

Cross-curricular activity/math

- Using a small balance scale, have children compare the weights of the rocks they brought in. Call on two volunteers to place their rocks on the balance scale. Have the class identify which rock is heavier. Call on two other children to display their rocks and ask the class to predict which one is heavier. Weigh the rocks on the balance scale. Continue in this manner until each child has had an opportunity to weigh his or her rock. Identify the heaviest rock and the lightest rock in the classroom. Then place the heaviest rock on the scale and have children predict how many lighter rocks it would take to equal the weight of the heaviest rock.

Home/school connections

- Suggest that children and their families collect four or five rocks. Ask them to compare the rocks and classify them according to color, size, and smoothness.
- Invite children to take the mini-book home to share with their families.

Non-fiction:

- Branley, Franklyn. *What the Moon Is Like*. Rev. ed. Illustrated by True Kelly. New York: HarperCollins, 1986.
- Cole, Joanna. *The Magic School Bus Out of This World: A Book about Space Rocks*. New York: Scholastic, 1996.
- Fowler, Alan. *It Could Still Be a Rock*. Chicago: Children's Press, 1993.
- Gans, Roma. *Rock Collecting*. Illustrated by Holly Keller. New York: HarperCollins, 1984.
- Hiscock, Bruce. *The Big Rock*. New York: Atheneum, 1988.
- Lunis, Natalie. *Rocks and Soil*. New York: Newbridge Educational Publishing, 1998.
- Marzollo, Jean. *I Am a Rock*. Illustrated by Judith Moffatt. New York: Scholastic 1998.

Fiction:

- Baylor, Byrd. *Everybody Needs a Rock*. Illustrated by Peter Parnall. New York: Macmillan, 1974.
- McDermott, Gerald. *The Stonecutter*. New York: Puffin, 1978.
- Steig, William. *Sylvester and the Magic Pebble*. New York: Simon & Schuster, 1980.

Snails in School!

Standards
Characteristics of organisms

Organisms and environments

Benchmarks
A lot can be learned about plants and animals by observing them closely, but care must be taken to know the needs of living things and how to provide for them in the classroom.

Supports
- headings
- some repetition of words and phrases

Challenges
- variety of sentence patterns

Text features
Punctuation: apostrophe

High-frequency words: *today, live, good, them, what, will, little, find, not*

Blends: *sm, sn, tw*

Digraphs: *ch, sh, wh*

Introducing the text
- Discuss the front- and back-cover photographs and ask children to work out the title.
- Have children draw on their knowledge and experience to talk about snails and what they might learn by caring for some snails in the classroom for several days.

The first reading

Contents page: Show children the contents page and read it with them. Have them speculate on how the book might progress based on the headings.

Pages 2-3: Model the heading and discuss how it helps organize the contents. Ask: *What will they do with the snails?* Have children read the page silently to find out.

Pages 4-5: Encourage children to use a range of problem-solving strategies to find out what the snails require to live.

Pages 6-10: Continue to briefly survey photographs and text to establish the organization of the book, and to

Today the snails came.

Pages 10-16: model syntactic structures and unfamiliar vocabulary. Have children continue to use a range of problem-solving strategies to monitor meaning.

Continue modeling structure and content by discussing the focus for each day and paying close attention to one or two details that challenge children to be active problem solvers.

The snail eats the lettuce. Lettuce helps it grow.

Ask children to turn to the front cover and to read aloud independently. Observe their strategies and behaviors. Are they using the organization of the book to support meaning? Are they confidently reading high-frequency words?

Rereading and discussing

- Discuss children's responses to the book. What new things did they learn about snails? Did the book remind them of other things they knew about snails? What else would they like to learn about snails?
- Discuss how the organization of the written text helped them to focus on meaning. Return to page 10 or page 14 to model how the introductory question helped their thinking.
- Have children buddy-read their books and use this time to observe their strategies.

Science connections

In this activity children will take care of and observe snails.

Materials: snails, disposable clear plastic food containers with holes punched in the top, lettuce, carrots, white chalk or cuttlebone, garlic, apple, lemon, sandpaper, plain paper, flashlight, black construction paper, tape, potting soil, twigs, small rocks, lids from juice bottles (for water), eye-droppers

Preparation: A few days before, order the snails. Connecticut Valley Biological Supply or Carolina Biological Supply are two sources for snails. Immediately unpack the snails when they arrive. Use tape and the black construction paper to make small cone-shaped tents. Cut a door at the bottom of each big enough for a snail.

Note: If during any of the activities a snail starts to foam, it is very important to quickly rinse it off in cool water.

The following activities may be done over a one-week period.

- Have each child put about an inch of potting soil in a container and add one or two rocks and twigs. Give a snail to each child. Have children name their snails. Label each container with the child's and snail's names. Place a bottle lid with water in each.

- Have children work in small groups. Provide each group with lettuce, carrot peels, small pieces of apple, a slice of lemon (cut up in 5 small pieces), a piece of chalk or cuttlebone, and a garlic clove (peeled and cut up in slivers). Tell children to place each food item in front of the snail's head to see if the snail will eat it. Have children record their findings.
- Distribute flashlights, black cones, sandpaper, and a sheet of drawing paper to each group. Have groups place a snail on the sandpaper and one on the drawing paper and observe what happens. Then have children place the cone on the drawing paper. The door side should be facing the snail. Have children shine the flashlight on the snail and observe what happens.

Reading and writing science

- Ask children to imagine they were going to leave their snails with a friend. Ask them what instructions the friend would need to follow to take care of their snails. Provide each child with a large index card. Have them write the care instructions on the card.

Cross-curricular activity/math

- Have children measure and weigh their snails and compare their findings. Help children line up the snails from the biggest to the smallest. You may also want to hold snail races. Have snails race the length of a piece of paper. Have children put three or four snails on one end and some carrot peels on the other end. Children might use a stopwatch to record the time of the fastest snail. Have children compare their findings.

Home/school connections

- After the snail investigation is completed, send the snails home with children. Be sure children take along the care directions they wrote. Encourage children to share what they have learned about snails with their families.
- Invite children to take the mini-book home to share with their families

Non-fiction:

- Greenberg, David. *Slugs*. Illustrated by Victoria Chase. Boston: Little, Brown/Joy Street Books, 1983.
- Zoehfeld, Kathleen Weidner. *What Lives in a Shell?* Illustrated by Helen Davie. New York: HarperCollins, 1994.

Fiction:

- Maccarone, Grace. *The Classroom Pet*. Illustrated by Betsy Lewin. New York: Scholastic, 1995.
- Schreiber, Anne. *Slower Than a Snail*. Illustrated by Larry Daste. New York: Scholastic, 1995.
- Stadler, John. *The Adventures of Snail at School.* New York: HarperCollins, 1993.

Up Close
A

Standards
Understands the nature of technological design

Benchmarks
Magnifiers help people see things they could not see without them.

Sometimes a person can get different information by moving closer or farther away.

Supports
- repetitive question/answer pattern
- repetitive language

Challenges
- complex sentence structures
- specialized language: *zebra, magnifying glass*

Text features
Punctuation: question and exclamation marks, apostrophe

High-frequency words: *you, what, this, look, when, new, will, made, here*

Blends: *cl, gl, gr, st, tr*

Digraphs: *th, wh*

Compound word: *strawberry*

Introducing the text
- Give each child a copy of the book. Tell them it is about seeing things up close through a magnifying glass. Establish that things in the book will appear larger and more detailed than they do in real life.
- Discuss what the close-up photographs could be on the front and back covers. Provide clues until the children are successful.

The first reading

Title page: Read the title page together. Confirm that the print is the same print as on the cover.

Pages 2–7: Survey the photographs together and establish the question-and-answer pattern by modeling the language in a conversational way.

Page 8: Ask: *What is the boy looking through?* Have children locate the word and discuss effective ways to work out the word. Ask: *What does it help you do?* Have

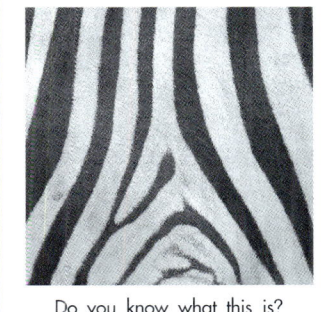

Do you know what this is? Look closely.

6

	children find and read the reply.
Page 9:	Say: *Read and find out what you learn when you look closely.*
Page 10:	Ask: *What part of the tree is this? Find a word to describe how it would feel.*
Pages 11-14:	Continue to survey the photographs and to model strategies for exploring the text.
Pages 15-16:	Ask: *Can you guess what this is?* Invite predictions before reading page 16.

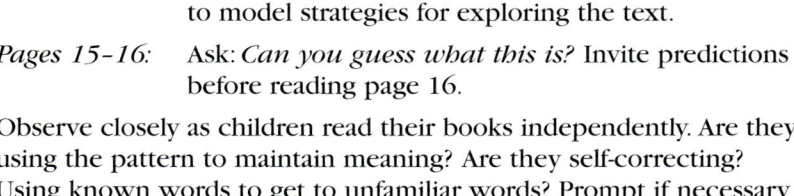

Look at this salt.

Observe closely as children read their books independently. Are they using the pattern to maintain meaning? Are they self-correcting? Using known words to get to unfamiliar words? Prompt if necessary and praise effective strategy use.

Rereading and discussing

- When children have finished, focus discussion on the content of the book. What did they find personally interesting? What would they like to observe through a magnifying glass?
- Discuss any parts of the book that children found challenging. What did they do to overcome challenges? What else could they do?
- Make the apostrophe *s* a brief teaching point.
- Have the children read their books again, independently or with a buddy.

Science connections

In this activity children will use a magnifying glass or microscope to view an assortment of objects.

Materials: For each group of five children you will need: a magnifying glass or microscope; assorted items, such as an insect wing, bird's feather, animal hair, leaf, thread, piece of bark; paper (folded in half); and pencils to record findings.

- Distribute the materials to each group. Briefly instruct children, if necessary, on the use of the microscope or magnifying glass.
- First ask children, one at a time, to examine the leaf without the microscope or magnifying glass. Call on one or two children to briefly describe the leaf. Then have children look at the leaf using the microscope or magnifying glass. Call on one or two children to describe what details they saw when they looked closely at the leaf.
- Have children work independently in groups to examine the remaining items. Then have each child choose one item. Have them draw a picture of what it looks like without magnification on the left side of their paper. Have them draw a picture of what it looks like magnified on the right side of their paper.

Reading and writing science

- Walk with children in the school playground. Ask each child to find a small item, such as a pebble, a few grains of sand, or a blade of grass. Back in the classroom have children use magnifying glasses or microscopes to look closely at their items. Write the following sentences on the board: *I looked closely at a (an)_____. I saw _____.*
- Have children use the sentences to write about their items. They may wish to include a drawing of the item as well. Display children's work on the bulletin board.

Cross-curricular activity/social studies

- With children, explore the many ways people use magnifying lenses, telescopes, microscopes, eyeglasses, binoculars, and loupes to look closely. Begin by discussing with children how eyeglasses can make the type bigger so that people can read it. Ask children to share any personal experiences if they care to. Discuss the following items and ask children how they might be used by people. (magnifying lens: used by doctors to see a splinter that needs to be removed; telescope: used to see the stars, used on a boat to look for land; microscope: used by scientists to look at germs or small organisms; binoculars: used by people to look at animals in nature, watch sports events; loupes: used by jewelers to look at stones or to work with a piece of jewelry.) Have children look through magazines to find pictures of people using a variety of magnifiers. Have children cut out the pictures. Use them to create a bulletin-board display titled, "People Who Look Closely."

Home/school connections

- Ask children and their families to look at a number of household items using a magnifying glass. Suggest they examine a sponge, steel wool, grains of sugar or salt, and breakfast cereal and identify what details they see. Allow time for children to share what item was their favorite and why.
- Invite children to take the mini-book home to share with their families.

Non-fiction:

- Hoban, Tana. *Look Again!* New York: Simon & Schuster, 1971.
- Sanved, Kjell Block. *Butterfly Alphabet.* New York: Scholastic, 1996.
- Selsam, Millicent. *Greg's Microscope.* New York: HarperCollins, 1963.

Fiction and poetry:

- Bruchac, Joseph. *The First Strawberries: A Cherokee Story.* Illustrated by Anna Vojtech. New York: Dial, 1995.
- Kumin, Maxine. *The Microscope.* Illustrated by Arnold Lobel. New York: HarperCollins, 1988.
- Sharmat, Marjorie Weinman. *Nate the Great and the Pillowcase.* Illustrated by Marc Simont. New York: Dell, 1993.
- Wood, Don and Audrey. *The Little Mouse, the Red Ripe Strawberry, and the Big Hungry Bear.* New York: Scholastic, 1995.

What Can Change?

Standards
Understands basic earth processes

Understands cycling of matter and flow of energy

Benchmarks
Change is something that happens to many things.

Changes happen in everyone's life.

Supports
- strong photo/text match
- familiar events

Challenges
- variety of sentence structures

Text features
Punctuation: question mark, ellipses

High-frequency words: *these, this, water, some, other, how*

Blends: *br, gr, pl, sm*

Introducing the text
- Discuss the front- and back-cover photographs. Ask what can change and have children find and read these words in the title.
- Draw on children's prior knowledge to brainstorm a list of things that can change. Begin by drawing their attention to their immediate surroundings before focusing on people, plants, animals, and changes brought about by the weather.

The first reading

Title page: Invite children to read the title and briefly talk about the photograph.

Page 2: Ask: *What change do you see here?* Have children silently read the words. Tell them that this is a way some informational books begin and remind them that they could use these words in their own writing.

Page 3: Ask: *How will these little chicks grow and change?*

Page 4: Ask them to read the words that tell what some chicks will become.

Pages 5–8: Continue to survey details in the photos and text to prompt them to problem-solve.

These little chicks will grow and change.

Page 9:	Model the language.
Page 10:	Ask them to read this page and find the answer.
Page 11:	Ask: *What do you notice about the first two words on this page?* Read the page together.
Pages 12-16:	Briefly survey these pages.

What will happen to this snow in the spring?

When you are confident that children can read the text for themselves, ask them to begin at the front cover and read aloud, independently. Do they recognize the same words in different sentence structures? Are they beginning to use phrasing?

Rereading and discussing

- Focus discussion on the children's individual responses to the book. What did they like? What questions do they have now?
- Ask them to look at page 2 and read it together. Briefly focus on the transitional language on pages 7 and 9. Challenge children to identify all the transitional words on pages 11 and 13.
- Ask children to buddy-read. Provide opportunities for them to reread their books over the next few days.

Science connections

In this activity children will explore how a lemon can change.

Materials: lemon, large glass jar with a screw-on lid, clear plastic cup (punch a hole in the bottom for drainage), soil, drawing materials

- Tell children they are going to observe a lemon over a ten-day period to see how it changes. Cut a wedge out of the lemon and remove a few of the seeds. Then place the lemon in the glass jar and replace the lid. Ask children to describe the lemon and then the lemon seed.
- Fill the plastic cup with soil. Plant the lemon seed $1^{1}/_{2}$ inches below the soil close to the side of the cup so that any growth can be seen. Water the seed and place the cup in a sunny window.
- Distribute drawing materials to children. Have them fold their papers in half. On one side have them draw the lemon and on the other half the lemon seed. Have them write *Day One* at the top of their papers.
- Each day, for the next nine days, have children examine the lemon and describe how it is changing. Every other day have them draw a picture of the lemon and of the lemon seed. (It may take a week for the lemon seed to sprout).
- After ten days, ask children to describe what the lemon looked like on the first day and to tell how it changed over the ten days. Do the same with the lemon seed. Ask volunteers to tell what they think will happen to the lemon and the seed over a period of time.

Reading and writing science

- First distribute drawing materials and have children illustrate how they think the lemon and the lemon seed will change next. Have them write a sentence about their drawings that describes each item. Before writing, review their responses on their charts. Encourage children to use these as a reference for their own writing. Provide time for children to share and read each other's books.
- Have children collect the drawings they did of the lemon and the lemon seed into a book of their own.

Cross-curricular activity/language arts/drama

Materials: colored construction paper, crayons, scissors, pipe cleaners

In this activity children will act out how things change.

- Divide children into several groups. Have each group select something that changes to act out. For instance, one group might pick the four seasons and each child in the group will "be" a season, acting out the effects of hot sun, snow, etc. Another group might show how a puppy changes, from birth to adult dog.
- Encourage children to create props and costumes (dog ears, green leaves, etc.) which will help them illustrate how things change.

Home/school connections

- Encourage children and their families to talk about the ways the adults in their families have changed since they were children. Suggest older family members share pictures of themselves when they were young. They might discuss not only the ways they changed physically, but also how they changed in terms of what they are able to do.
- Invite children to take the mini-book home to share with their families.

Non-fiction:

- Aliki. *I'm Growing!* New York: HarperTrophy, 1993.
- Allen, Marjorie N., and Shelly Rotner. *Changes*. New York: Aladdin, 1993.
- Gomi, Taro. *Spring Is Here*. San Francisco: Chronicle Books, 1994.
- Maestro, Betsy. *Why Do Leaves Change Color?* Illustrated by Loretta Krupinski. New York: HarperTrophy, 1994.

Fiction:

- Bates, Lucy. *Little Rabbit's Loose Tooth*. New York: Crown, 1983.
- Hutchins, Pat. *You'll Soon Grow into Them, Titch*. New York: Greenwillow, 1983.
- Keats, Ezra Jack. *Peter's Chair*. New York: HarperTrophy: 1983.

What Does a Garden Need? A

Standards
Knows the general structure and functions of cells in organisms

Benchmarks
To grow well, plants need warmth, light, and water.

Supports
- strong photo/text match
- repetitive language

Challenges
- specialized vocabulary: *bulbs, dirt*

Text features
Punctuation: question mark

High-frequency words: *people, garden, some, other, from, grow, need, little*

Blends: *fl, pl*

Introducing the text
- Discuss the front- and back-cover photographs. Tell children the name of the book.
- Draw on children's prior knowledge by asking them to share what they know about gardens. End the discussion by listing the essentials for establishing a garden.

The first reading
Invite children to read the title and talk about the photographs.

Title page: Have children look at the photograph and talk about it.

Pages 2-9: Ask children to briefly survey each photograph to find what a garden needs. Model the predictable text pattern that introduces each new element and draw attention to the use of the words *some* and *other* as comparisons. Engage children in different ways of predicting and confirming meaning by checking details in the print, checking to see if it makes sense, and checking that it sounds right.

Pages 10-11: Ask: *What does a garden need now?*

People use tools to dig up dirt.

	Model *What if there is no rain?* Have children find out and read the answer.
Pages 12-15:	Briefly discuss photographs and text.
Page 16:	Have children read this page independently.

What if there is no rain? People can water their gardens.

When you are confident that the children have sufficient information to read the book independently, ask them to return to the front of the book and read it themselves. Observe children as they read at the same time, but independently of each other. Are they using the repetitive language effectively? Focusing on meaning? Using several sources of information to self-correct?

Rereading and discussing

- Invite responses to the book. What questions do children have after reading the book?
- Focus further discussion on effective strategies you observed children using. Then focus briefly on how the words *some* and *other* were used to compare and contrast.
- Ask children to reread their books. Provide opportunities for them to read the book again independently over the next few days.

Science connections

In this activity children will grow bean plants and will draw conclusions about what plants need to grow well.

Materials: For each child: large paper drinking cup, soil, bean seed

- Call on children to talk about the book *What Does a Garden Need?* Ask them to recall the things a garden needs to grow well. As children make suggestions, write their responses on chart paper. Tell children that they are going to grow their own bean plants to discover what a garden needs.
- Distribute the cups, bean seeds, and soil to children. Have them fill their cups 3/4 full with soil and make a hole about 2 inches deep. Drop in the bean seed and cover with soil. Have children sprinkle water on the newly planted seeds (about an ounce for each cup). Place the cups on the classroom windowsill (not over heaters) where they can get enough sunlight. Prepare 2 or 3 cups yourself for classroom experiments.
- Ask children to observe the plants as they grow. Have children water their plants, when needed. Review with children that plants need sunlight to grow. Tell them that the class will do an experiment to see if this is true. Line the inside of a brown paper bag with black construction paper and place over one of the bean plants. Remove the bag every day and have children observe what is happening to the plant.
- Review with children that plants need water to grow. Tell them they will also do an experiment to see if this is true. Stop watering one of the bean plants. Look at the plant every day.

Have children observe what happens to the plant when it does not get water.
- Review with children what a garden needs to grow. If possible, have children plant their bean plants outdoors, where they can watch them grow, flower, and produce beans.

Reading and writing science

- Have children keep a daily journal in which they record the progress of their bean plants. Suggest children draw pictures of their plants and write a sentence or two describing them. Encourage children to use adjectives when describing their plants. You may want to brainstorm with children to come up with descriptive words. Keep a list of these words on a word wall so that children can refer to them.

Cross-curricular activity/math

Materials: household string, legal-size paper

- Help children make "string" graphs to record the growth of their plants. Take legal-size sheets of paper and draw a line across the bottom of a short side. Hold the paper the long way and make marks about an inch apart across the line. Every two or three days have children measure their plants with string and cut the string to the height of the plant. Then show children how to tape the string to the paper and write the date beneath the mark. After a week or so have children display their graphs and compare and comment on the rate at which their plants are growing.

Home/school connections

- Encourage children and their families to plant or purchase a small plant to keep and observe at home. In this way the concept that a plant needs soil, water, sunlight, and warmth to grow will be reinforced.
- Invite children to take the mini-book home to share with their families.

Non-fiction:

- Berger, Melvin. *The Vegetable Garden.* New York: Newbridge Educational Publishing, 1995.
- Burns, Diane. *Wildflowers, Blooms, and Blossoms.* Minnetonka, MN: NorthWind Press, 1997.
- Carle, Eric. *The Tiny Seed.* New York: Scholastic, 1990.
- Ehlert, Lois. *Planting a Rainbow.* San Diego: Harcourt, 1988.
- Maas, Robert. *Garden.* New York: Henry Holt, 1998.

Fiction:

- Bunting, Eve. *Flower Garden.* Illustrated by Katherine Hewitt. San Diego: Harcourt, 1994.
- DiSalvo-Ryan, Dianne. *City Green.* New York: Morrow, 1994.
- Hall, Zoe. *The Surprise Garden.* Illustrated by Shari Halpern. New York: Scholastic, 1998.
- MacDonald, Margaret. *Pickin' Peas.* Illustrated by Pat Cummings. New York: HarperCollins, 1998.

Where Are the Eggs?

Standards
Knows about the diversity and unity that characterize life

Benchmarks
Living things have offspring, usually with two parents involved.

Supports
- repetitive language and sentence structures
- moderate to strong photo/text match

Challenges
- change in sentence pattern on pages 13, 14, 15, 16
- specialized vocabulary: *alligator, robin, turtle*

Text features
Punctuation: question mark

High-frequency words: *here, they, are, their, this, some, where, will, make, keep*

Blends: *th, wh*

Introducing the text
- Distribute books.
- Tell children this book is about animals who lay eggs, and the different places they choose to keep the eggs safe.
- Discuss the front- and back-cover photographs.
- Brainstorm egg-laying animals the children know. Where do they hide their eggs?

The first reading

Title page: Read the title page together and note where the eggs are.

Page 2: Model *Some animals lay eggs*. Have children locate the word *eggs*. Ask children to find and read the words that tell where animals lay their eggs.

Page 3: Ask what bird children see. Say: *Where will this robin…* Have

Some animals lay eggs. They lay their eggs in many different places.

children complete the question.

Page 4: Look at the photograph. Model the language.

Page 5: Have children locate and read the word *goose*.

Page 6: Ask where the goose will lay her eggs. Have children check the text to find out.

He keeps the egg warm until it hatches into a baby penguin.

Pages 7-12: Continue to build a framework by having children identify each new animal and where she has laid her eggs by checking details in photographs and text.

Page 13: Ask where this penguin will lay her egg. Have children read the text to find out.

Page 14: Ask where the egg is now. Have children check the photograph, then find the words that tell.

Page 15: Survey the photograph to see why the father penguin has the egg.

Page 16: Ask: *Who takes care of eggs so babies hatch and grow?*

Rereading and discussing

- Ask the children to read the book again, this time aloud and independently.
- Observe them, prompting where necessary to help them regain or maintain meaning. Are they using the pattern of the text to read with phrasing? Are they recognizing the same words in different sentence patterns?
- Share responses to the book. What did they learn? What did they like? Were there any tricky parts in the text? How did they figure them out?
- Comment positively on effective strategies children employ.
- Have children read the book with a buddy. Observe again. Provide opportunities for children to read their book again over the next few days.

Science connections

In this activity children will learn about the different kinds of animal families.

Materials: a variety of pictures of animal families—herds, single parents (male sea horse, mother bears with cubs), partners

- Talk with children about the animals they met in *Where Are the Eggs?* Have them name some of the animals from the book, where they laid their eggs, and how they cared for their eggs. Point out to children that in some animal families, such as robin and penguin families, the two parents care for the chicks when the eggs hatch.

In other animal families, such as alligator families, only the mother cares for the babies when the eggs hatch. With some animals, such as butterflies and turtles, the eggs are left to hatch. When the babies are born, they must learn to survive by themselves.
- Display a picture of a herd of elephants. Explain to children that a herd is one kind of animal family. In a herd, animals travel together to find food. Because there are many animals, they have more protection. Ask children what other animals live in herds. Write their responses on the board.
- Display pictures of other animal families, and discuss with children how they are special. Have children suggest other animals that live in these types of families.

Reading and writing science

- Make a bulletin board display entitled "Animal Families." Call on children to find pictures of a variety of animal families to add to the display. Each child should write on an index card a sentence that tells something about the animal family and attach it to the picture.

Cross-curricular activity/math

- Make a bar graph on a large sheet of chart paper. In the left column of the graph list the names of the animals children met in *Where Are the Eggs?* Elicit from children that some animals lay more eggs than others and that you are going to compare the number of eggs laid by each animal. Have children find the picture of the hen on page 2 of their books and count the eggs they see. Call on two volunteers to each draw an egg next to *hen*. Continue in the same way with the other animals in the book. (For the turtle, have children estimate the number of eggs.) When children have finished, pose questions that will help them compare the number of eggs each animal laid. For example, which animal(s) laid the greatest number of eggs? Which animal(s) laid the least?

Home/school connections

- Encourage children to note where animals or insects have laid eggs in their neighborhood and to record this information in writing and drawing. Suggest that they involve family members in their search.
- Invite children to take the mini-book home to share with their families.

Non-fiction:

- Arnosky, Jim. *All about Alligators*. New York: Scholastic, 1994.
- Burton, Jane, and Kim Taylor. *Egg*. New York: DK Publishing, 1997.
- Florian, Douglas. *Discovering Butterflies*. New York: Aladdin, 1990.
- Jenkins, Priscilla B. *A Nest Full of Eggs.* Illustrated by Lizzy Rockwell. New York: HarperCollins, 1995.

Fiction:

- Joyce, William. *Bently & Egg*. New York: HarperCollins, 1992.
- Lionni, Leo. *An Extraordinary Egg*. New York: Knopf, 1994.
- McCloskey, Robert. *Make Way for Ducklings*. New York: Viking, 1969.

Animals Build   Set B

Standards
Organisms and environments

Characteristics of organisms

Benchmarks
Animals and plants sometimes change their surroundings and objects can be described in terms of materials they are made of (clay, cloth, paper, etc.) and their physical properties (color, size, shape, weight, etc.).

Supports
- consistent print placement
- repetition of language

Challenges
- specialized vocabulary: *termites, mounds, chimpanzee, lodge*
- complex sentence structures

Text features
Punctuation: comma, exclamation point

Blends: *br, gr, sl, sp, st, tr, tw*

Digraphs: *ch, th*

Introducing the text
- Give each child a copy of the book.
- Discuss the front- and back-cover photographs and have children work out the title.
- Brainstorm other structures animals build and the materials they use to build them.

The first reading

Contents page: Introduce children to a table of contents. Have children read the page numbers given and ask them what they think they will find on that page. Use photos to check children's predictions.

Pages 2-3: Survey the photographs together. Establish that the beaver is building a lodge. Have children check the text to find out what beavers use to build lodges.

Pages 4-5: Ask: *Who can build here?* Model how to use *beaver* to work out *weaver*. Ask: *Can you see what the nests are made of?*

The lodges are made of sticks and mud.

3

	Have children check photograph and text to confirm their predictions.
Pages 6-13:	Continue to survey the photographs and text, modeling syntactic structures and unfamiliar language in a conversational way. Model a range of strategies to check predictions. *Does it make sense? If it was the word you thought it was, what letter does it begin with?*
Pages 14-15:	Say: *Spiders can build, too.* Ask children what spider webs feel like and why they are sticky before checking their replies against the text.
Page 16:	Survey the photograph. Briefly discuss why animals build, and check the text to confirm children's suggestions.

These webs are traps! Spiders use webs to catch food.

Have children read the book aloud at the same time. Observe the strategies for maintaining meaning: Are children using known words as anchors to work out unknown words? Are they focusing on meaning? Aware of, and using punctuation?

Rereading and discussing

- Comment positively on effective strategies and prompt only when needed.
- After children have read the book, focus a brief discussion on the parts they particularly liked and what they learned. What questions do they have now? If appropriate, make commas a teaching point, or model a strategy or skill.
- Have children buddy-read their books and use this time to observe their strategies.

Science connections

In this activity children will use a variety of materials to create a home for an animal.

Materials: modeling clay, cloth, paper, twigs, leaves, cotton balls, scissors, glue, tape

- Ask each child to think of an animal. Then ask them to think about a home they could build for the animal. What would the home look like? What materials would they use? After children have shared their ideas, tell them they will have the opportunity of making their own animal home using a variety of materials.
- Have children work individually or with a partner. Allow them time to build their animal homes. Provide assistance as necessary.
- When they are finished, call on children to describe the animal home they made.

Reading and writing science

- Take a short walk with children to a nearby park to identify the animals that live there. Talk about where each animal lives and the type of home each animal makes. Identify the materials the home is made of. Have children describe the materials, putting emphasis on their physical properties—color, weight, texture, etc. Back in the classroom, have children draw pictures of the things they saw. Help children label their drawings.

Cross-curricular activity/math

- Have children look around the classroom to find items made of wood and items made of metal. Make a simple bar graph on a sheet of chart paper with two columns, one labeled "Metal Items" and one labeled "Wooden Items". Tell children that each square on the bar graph stands for one item. Call on children, one at a time, to name an item made either of wood or metal. Have the child color in one square on the appropriate column of the bar graph. Continue until each child has had an opportunity to name an item. Ask the following questions and have children use the graph to answer them: *How many wooden items did the class identify? How many metal items did the class identify? Is there more of one kind of item than another? How many more?*

Home/school connections

- Provide each child with a large index card. Ask children and their families to look through a magazine or catalog to find an item that would be fun to describe. Have them cut out and glue the picture to one side of the index card. On the other side have them write what materials the item is made of, its color, size, and whether it's heavy or light. Distribute the cards to small groups of children. Have them read the clues and guess what the object is, then turn the card over to see if they're right.
- Invite children to take the mini-book home to share with their families.

Non-fiction:

- Bernhard, Emery. *Eagles: Lions of the Sky*. New York: Holiday House, 1994.
- Gibbons, Gail. *Spiders*. New York: Holiday House, 1993.
- Kitchen, Bert. *And So They Build*. Cambridge, MA: Candlewick, 1993.
- Lane, Margaret. *Beaver*. New York: Penguin, 1993.

Fiction:

- Edwards, Pamela Duncan. *Livingstone Mouse*. Illustrated by Henry Cole. New York: HarperCollins, 1996.
- Fleming, Denise. *Where Once There Was a Wood*. New York: Henry Holt, 1997.
- Polacco, Patricia. *The Bee Tree*. New York: Putnam, 1993.

At the Science Center

Standards
Understands the nature of scientific inquiry

Benchmarks
People can often learn about things around them by just observing those things carefully, but sometimes they learn more by doing something to those things and noting what happens to them.

Supports
- consistent layout
- repetition of opening sentence

Challenges
- specialized language
- variety of sentence structures

Text features
High-frequency words: *will, write, work, these, about, what, find, there, we, look*

Blends: *dr, fl, sm*

Compound word: *cannot*

Introducing the text
- Look at the photograph on the cover. Ask where these children are working and challenge the class to cross-check between text and photograph to read the title themselves.
- Talk about the kinds of activities children do in their science center, the tools they use to help them, and the ways they record their data.

The first reading

Title page: Read and discuss the title.

Pages 2–3: Have children silently read to find out what the children are saying.

Pages 4–7: Briefly survey these pages, helping children to identify and problem-solve unfamiliar vocabulary and a range of sentence structures in context.

Pages 8–9: Ask: *What will the students do to find out about the water?*

Pages 10–11: Have children silently read to find out what questions the children have about the rock and cork.

What will we find out about these shells? We can sort them.

4

Pages 12-16: Continue surveying the photographs and text, prompting children to problem-solve for themselves.

When you are satisfied that the children have sufficient information to read the book on their own, ask them to read independently while you observe. Are they recognizing the same words and phrases in a variety of sentence structures? Analyzing unfamiliar words and checking that they make sense?

Rereading and discussing

- Invite responses to the book. Do students have any questions? What did they learn? Make a teaching point if appropriate. Ask children to read their book with a partner.

Science connections

With this project, children will participate in a variety of science activities.

Materials: collection of shells, rocks, microscope, magnifying glass, variety of slides, cork, balance scale, several clear containers of different shapes, measuring cup, beakers or drinking glasses of varying sizes

Preparation: Set up a single science center or a number of different stations where children can duplicate the activities shown in *At the Science Center.* Call on children to bring in nature books and magazines, shells, rocks, feathers, old birds' nests, and other items from home.

- Set up the following stations:
  1. *Shells*: Provide shells of varying types, sizes, and colors. Have children sort them according to type, color, and size. Have them put the largest shell in the one dish of the balance scale and balance it with a number of small shells in the other dish. Provide children with simple worksheets to record their findings.
  2. *Water*: Provide children with a measuring cup, and glasses of varying shapes and sizes. Have children pour one cup of water into each container. Have them observe the level of the water in each and record their findings.
  3. *Float or Sink*: Have children test various items to see if they will float. Provide children with two glasses of water and a variety of items, including a rock, a cork, a leaf, a paper clip, a bottlecap, and so on. Have children test each item and record their findings.
  4. *Microscope/Magnifying Glass*: Have children examine a variety of items from nature using a microscope or magnifying glass. Have children draw a picture of an item and then look at the

item under the microscope or magnifying glass. Have them draw the magnified item.
- Have children work in groups at each station. Give children 15-20 minutes at each station and then have them switch. After children have completed the activities, give them time to discuss their findings.

Reading and writing science

- Explain to children that scientists often keep journals in which they write about what they observe, and that they often draw pictures to illustrate what they have seen. Write a model of a journal page on the chalkboard. Include the date, the time (clock face), the temperature (thermometer) and the weather (sun, cloud, rain). Draw a simple picture of a possible observation—for example, a squirrel cracking open a nut. Write two or three simple sentences describing the observation. Then have children begin their own journal pages.

Cross-curricular activity/art

Materials: Pictures of a cat, a land snail, a bicycle, a cross-section of an apple

- Tell children an important part of scientific investigation is recording observations. Remind children that scientists often draw and label diagrams showing their findings. Draw a simple diagram of a flower, including its stem, leaves, and roots. Call upon children to name the parts of the flower. Label the petals, stem, leaves, and roots. Display the pictures. Ask children to name some of the parts in each picture that could be labeled. Provide children with paper and have them choose one picture to draw and label. When children have completed the assignment, have them display their diagrams to the class.

Home/school connections

- Encourage children and their families to create their own nature journals. Suggest they take a nature walk, make observations, and record what they see.
- Invite children to take the mini-book home to share with their families.

Non-fiction:

- Bennett, Andrea. *Apples, Bubbles, and Crystals: Your Science ABCs*. New York: McGraw-Hill, 1996.
- *DK Finders: Young Scientist*. New York: DK Publishing, 1997.
- Patchett, Lynne. *My Shell*. New York: Orchard, 1995.
- Rowe, Julian. *Keep It Afloat!* Chicago: Children's Press, 1993.

Fiction:

- Bourgeois, Paulette. *Too Many Chickens!* Illustrated by Bill Slavin. Boston: Little Brown, 1991.
- Keenan, Sheila. *More or Less a Mess.* Illustrated by Patrick Girouard. New York: Scholastic, 1997.

The Coral Reef   B

Standards
Understands how species depend on one another and the environment for survival

Benchmarks
Living things are found almost everywhere in the world.

Plants and animals have features that help them live in different environments.

Animals use plants (or even other animals) for shelter and nesting.

Supports
- moderate to strong photo/text match
- repetitive patterns

Challenges
- variety of print placements
- complex sentence structures
- specialized language: *tentacles, clownfish, octopus*

Text features
Punctuation: comma, apostrophe

High-frequency words: *here, this, can, you, live, blue, black, when*

Blends: *bl, cl, gr*

Introducing the text

- Distribute a book to each child in the group. Tell the children the new book is called *The Coral Reef*. Through discussion of the cover photographs, establish that the coral reef is made up of many tiny animals called corals, and that many fish and other animals also live in the reef.

The first reading

Title page: Read the title page together and identify the sea anemones.

Pages 2-3: Survey the photograph. Model *This is a coral reef.* Ask children to find the words *coral reef*, then read the next two lines to find out what the reef is made up of. Model *Many other sea animals live on the reef, too.*

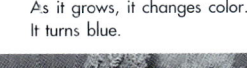
As it grows, it changes color. It turns blue.

71

	Then say: *Let's look at the photographs to see some of them.*
Pages 4-5:	Ask: *Can you find the name of this fish? What happens as it grows bigger?*
Pages 6-7:	Say: *These fish stay near an animal with green tentacles. Can you find their name?* Have children read page 7 to find out why they hide in the tentacles.
Pages 8-15:	Continue discussing the photographs, drawing children's attention to the structure of the text, the layout, and some of the new and challenging vocabulary and concepts. Help children use what they already know.
Page 16:	Ask: *Whom do you see? What is the diver doing?* Have children read the last two lines to check predictions. Then ask: *What do you think he will photograph next?*

The animals of the coral reef are amazing.
What will the diver photograph next on the coral reef?

16

Ask children to read the book aloud independently. Observe their strategies and behaviors. Are they recognizing and using the layout to predict content and meaning? Rereading to check and confirm? Analyzing new words and checking that they sound right and make sense?

Rereading and discussing

- Discuss particular pages children enjoyed most. What have they learned?
- Would they like to know more about any of the animals?
- Identify one or two challenging pieces of text and share strategies for working them out.
- Point out the different ways the apostrophes have been used on pages 9 and 13.
- Buddy-read, taking turns through several pages at a time.

Science connections

In this activity children will make observations in a local park or the neighborhood to identify the animals that live there.

- Remind children that the coral reef is home to many different kinds of animals. Call on children to name some of the animals and describe what they look like, the food they eat, and where in the reef they can be found.
- Tell children that the neighborhood they live in is home to many different kinds of animals, too. Have children briefly describe the plants and animals that can be found in a nearby park or in the neighborhood. Take a walk to the park or around the neighborhood to observe the animals that live there. Have children

find and observe three or four animals (such as birds, squirrels, worms, caterpillars, and so on). Have them describe what each animal looks like and identify the food each animal eats, the place where each animal lives, and any other interesting information they gather while observing the animal.
- Back in the classroom, discuss children's observations about each animal. Call on volunteers to act out a behavior they observed—a squirrel hopping along the ground, a bird bobbing as it walks, a worm moving along a rock.

Reading and writing science
- Have children play a riddle game. Ask each child to choose an animal and write three descriptive clues about the animal, such as its color, where it lives, what it eats, or who its enemies are. Invite children, one at a time, to tell their clues to the class. After each clue is read, give the class two chances to guess the animal. After the animal is identified, allow children to share what information they have about the animal.

Cross-curricular activity/art
- On a large sheet of chart paper, create a very sparse scene of a local habitat. Invite children to add plants and animals to the mural. Suggest children draw pictures of plants or animals or find pictures in magazines to cut out. As children add to the mural, discuss each addition with them. Ask questions such as: *Jeanie added a frog. What color is this frog? Where does the frog live? What kind of food do you think the frog eats? How does the frog move? Do you think the frog has any enemies? What animals might they be?*

Home/school connections
- Suggest that children and their families visit a habitat near their homes to observe animals there. Have families find three or four different animals, draw pictures of them, and write a sentence or two about each animal. Allow time for children to share their observations with the group.
- Invite children to take the mini-book home to share with their families.

Non-fiction:
- Berger, Melvin. *Life in a Coral Reef.* New York: Newbridge Educational Publishing, 1994.
- Brenner, Barbara, and Bernice Chardiet. *Where's That Fish?* Illustrated by Carol Schwartz. New York: Scholastic, 1994.
- Dunphy, Madeline. *Here Is the Coral Reef.* Illustrated by Tom Leonard. New York: Hyperion, 1998.
- Lauber, Patricia. *An Octopus Is Amazing.* Illustrated by Holly Keller. New York: HarperCollins, 1990.
- Wu, Norbert. *Fish Faces.* New York: Henry Holt, 1993.

Fiction:
- Aliki. *My Visit to the Aquarium.* New York: HarperCollins, 1993.
- Lionni, Leo. *Swimmy.* New York: Knopf, 1991.

Corn: From Farm to Table

Standards
Abilities of technological design

Characteristics of organisms

Benchmarks
Machines improve what people reap from crops—by helping in planting and harvesting, and in transporting it long distances.

Supports
- sequence of events
- moderate photo/text match

Challenges
- variety of sentence structures
- specialized language
- labeled diagram

Text features
Punctuation: colon

High-frequency words: *for, you, of, this, with, good, make, eat, many, made*

Blends: *dr, pl, sp, st, tr*

Introducing the text
- Talk about the cover photographs, focusing discussion on where corn grows and how it is used.
- Tell children the title and read it together. Ask them to predict what they will find out about corn in the book. Briefly discuss how corn is grown and harvested, and machines that help do this.

The first reading

Title page: Read the title page together and note the photograph.

Pages 2-3: Briefly survey the photographs to establish who grows corn and who eats it.

Pages 4-8: Browse through these pages, identifying the machines and how they help at each stage of the corn's growth. Model unfamiliar language in the discussion and prompt children to use a variety of problem-solving approaches, including making predictions and drawing conclusions based on

Farms use machines to water corn. This machine sprays water on the corn.

7

Pages 9-13: the meaning of the print photographs.

Continue to discuss the photographs and text as you help children build a framework for reading the book independently.

Pages 14-15: Show children how the diagram works and read one or two of the headings.

Page 16: Ask children what corn products they eat for breakfast.

This tractor takes ears of corn to the market.

Ask children to read aloud independently. Observe their strategies and behaviors. How are they solving unfamiliar words? Are they using photographs and text in an integrated way? Are they monitoring meaning?

Rereading and discussing

- Share children's responses. What did they learn about? What did they particularly like? What would they like to find out more about?
- Focus discussion on their strategies. What were the tricky words? What did they do to keep reading? Comment on the use of effective strategies and behavior you observed.
- Provide opportunities for them to read the book again over the next few days.

Science connections

In this activity children will examine a variety of simple machines to learn how machines make work easier.

Materials: rulers, books, small boxes, round cylinders, wooden blocks

- Demonstrate the use of a lever, plane, and wheels for children. Then distribute materials and have children experiment with these machines in small groups. Write the word *lever* on the chalkboard. Place a book on the table in front of you and ask a child to lift one end off the table. Point out that lifting the book is work. Then place a wooden block on the table (to act as the fulcrum) and put the ruler on top of it. Explain that the ruler will act as a lever to lift the book and make the work easier. Put the end of the ruler under the book. Demonstrate how to push down on the other end of the ruler to lift the book. Call on a volunteer to repeat the demonstration.
- Then demonstrate the use of a plane to children. Put a stack of books on the table in front of you. Place a block of wood near them. Lift the block and place it on top of the stack. Elicit from children that this action is work. Take a book and lean it against the stack of books to make a plane. Write the word *plane* on the

board. Call on a volunteer to push the block of wood up the plane to the top of the stack of books. Discuss that the plane has made the work easier.
- Finally, demonstrate the use of wheels to children. Write the word *wheels* on the chalkboard. Place a box on the table and push it along. Then place two cylinders under the box. Call on a volunteer to push the box. Have children observe how easily the box moves along the tabletop.
- Discuss with children when they have seen these machines at work. You may want to suggest a wheelchair ramp (plane), or a screwdriver used to open a paint can or pry open a box (lever).
- Allow time for children to experiment with the devices.

Reading and writing science
- Have children look through magazines to find examples of machines at work. Have them cut out the pictures and glue them onto a sheet of construction paper. Call upon children to display their pictures. Then have them name the machine and describe the work the machine does. Ask children to write the name of the machine and a sentence telling what work the machine does under the picture. Display the pictures on the bulletin board.

Cross-curricular activity/social studies
- Tell children they will take a walk in the school neighborhood to find machines at work. As you walk with children, have them point out the various machines they see and identify the jobs they do. Back in the classroom have children talk about the machines they saw and the jobs they did. Have each child draw a picture of one of the machines and write the name beneath it.

Home/school connections
- Encourage children and their families to talk about the machines they use at home and the jobs the machines do. Invite children to draw and write about one machine. Share these drawings with the group.
- Invite children to take the mini-book home to share with their families.

Non-fiction:
- Aliki. *Corn Is Maize*. New York: HarperTrophy, 1976.
- Berger, Melvin. *From Peanuts to Peanut Butter.* New York: Newbridge Educational Publishing, 1992.
- Fowler, Alan. *Corn—On and Off the Cob*. Danbury, CT: Children's Press, 1994.
- McMillan, Bruce. *Jelly Beans for Sale*. New York: Scholastic, 1996.
- Royston, Angela. *Truck Trouble*. New York: DK Publishing, 1998.

Fiction:
- Gerson, Mary-Joan. *People of the Corn: A Mayan Story*. Illustrated by Cara Golembe. Boston: Little, Brown, 1995.
- Johnston, Tony. *We Love the Dirt*. Illustrated by Alexa Brandenberg. New York: Scholastic, 1997.
- Low, Alice. *The Popcorn Shop*. Illustrated by Patti Hammel.

From the Earth   B

Standards
Understands energy types, sources, and conversions

Benchmarks
People burn fuels such as wood, oil, coal, and natural gas, or use electricity to cook their food and warm their homes.

Supports
- repetitive text structure
- consistent layout

Challenges
- contents page
- specialized language

Text features
Punctuation: ellipses

High-frequency words: *we, make, from, that, get, trees, how, use, they, many, some*

Digraphs: *ch, th*

Introducing the text
- Tell children the book is called *From the Earth* and is about things people use from the earth to cook, heat their homes, and help make electricity.
- Identify and discuss what is being used in the cover photographs and brainstorm other ways to use wood and water.

The first reading

Contents page: Talk about the photographs, and match each to the natural resource it illustrates. Read the contents page together.

Pages 2-5: Read the heading. Model the introductory and last sentences. Briefly survey the photographs and text to establish the layout and the text pattern and to introduce unfamiliar vocabulary through discussion.

Pages 6-9: Continue to survey text and photographs, modeling content and structure through discussion.

Pages 10-11: Challenge children to read the heading and to find what power plants and dams use to make electricity.

Page 12: Ask children to look at the photograph and

We get wood from trees.
Wood can be used in many ways.

	read the page silently to find out what power lines do.
Pages 13-16:	Read the sentence on page 13 together. Survey the remaining pages briefly.

When you have built a sufficient framework for the children to read the books independently, ask them to return to the front cover and read for themselves.

Dams use water to help make electricity.

Rereading and discussing

- Observe children as they read their books independently. Are they checking meaning from multiple sources of information? Using the text pattern to maintain momentum? Using phrasing? Self-correcting?
- Praise effective strategies and support independent problem-solving.
- Browse through some of the pages, inviting children to raise new questions about the content. Focus on any tricky words that they identify.
- Have them buddy-read the text.

Science connections

- In this activity children will explore how wood, oil, and electricity are used in their daily lives.
- Ask children to recall what they read in *From the Earth*. Ask them to name some of the uses of wood, oil, and electricity mentioned in the book. Write their responses on the chalkboard. Call on volunteers to give other examples of the uses for wood, oil, and electricity. Tell children they will investigate how wood, oil, and electricity are used in their daily lives.
- Make a chart entitled "From the Earth." Make three columns labeled "Wood," "Oil," and "Electricity." Ask children to look around the classroom to find items made of wood or wood products. Have children name the items and list them under the "Wood" column.
- Take children on a walk through the school and the school grounds to find examples of how oil and electricity are used in their daily lives. List children's responses on the chart.
- Explain to children that wood, oil, and water (to run power plants that produce electricity) are natural resources. Discuss with children why it would be important to protect these resources.

Reading and writing science

- Find a picture in a magazine that shows how natural resources are utilized (for example, a family sitting in front of a fireplace, reading by the light of a lamp). Display the picture and have children tell how natural resources are being used. Then have children, working with a partner, look through magazines to find a picture on their own. Have children identify how oil, wood, or electricity are utilized and write a phrase or sentence on a large index card. Provide

assistance as necessary. Have partners present their work to the class. Display the pictures and the index cards on the bulletin board.
- Point out to children that wood is also used to make paper. Ask children to brainstorm some paper products that they use in school and at home. Write them on the chalkboard. Have each child choose two paper products that they use and write a sentence about each. Have children read and discuss their sentences with the class.

Cross-curricular activity/math

- Discuss with children that they often use the electricity generated by electric batteries when they play. Have each child think of a favorite toy and decide if it uses an electric plug, a battery, or neither one.
- Make a graph entitled "How Our Toys Run" (see diagram). Then call on children one at a time to name their toy, see if it needs a battery, an electric plug, or neither, and color the square in the appropriate column. Have children use the graph to make comparisons.

HOW OUR TOYS RUN			
NAME OF TOY	BATTERY	ELECTRIC PLUG	NEITHER

Home/school connections

- Encourage children and their families to look for ways they use wood, oil, and electricity. Suggest that families keep a list and add to it as they find more examples.
- Invite children to take the mini-book home to share with their families.

Non-fiction:

- Cole, Joanna. *The Magic School Bus and the Electric Field Trip*. Illustrated by Bruce Degen. New York: Scholastic, 1997.
- Gibbons, Gail. *Fill It Up! A Book About Service Stations*. New York: HarperCollins, 1985.
- Lauber, Patricia. *Be a Friend to Trees*. Illustrated by Holly Keller. New York: HarperCollins, 1994.
- Oppenheim, Joanne. *Have You Seen Trees?* New York: Scholastic, 1995.

Fiction:

- Cherry, Lynne. *The Great Kapok Tree*. San Diego: Harcourt Brace, 1990.
- Stolz, Mary. *Storm at Night*. Illustrated by Pat Cummings. New York: HarperCollins, 1990.
- Udry, Janice May. *A Tree Is Nice*. Illustrated by Marc Simont. New York: HarperCollins, 1984.

Fur, Feathers, Scales, Skin

Standards
Understands how species depend on one another and on the environment for survival

Benchmarks
Different plants and animals have external features that help them thrive in different kinds of places.

Supports
- familiar animals
- moderate photo/text support

Challenges
- variety of sentence structures
- headings

Text features
Punctuation: apostrophe

High-frequency words: *some, many, have, help, are, keep, same, from, gets, good, back*

Digraphs: *ph, sh, th, wh*

Blends: *sc, sk, sm, th*

Letter cluster: *scr*

Compound word: *something*

Introducing the text
- Distribute a book to each child. Tell them the book is about the different coverings animals have and is called *Fur, Feathers, Scales, Skin*. Which ones can they find in the cover photos?
- Brainstorm other animals that have these coverings, and discuss how the coverings help the animals survive in their environment.

The first reading

Pages 2-3: Note the heading and read it together. Discuss how headings help readers anticipate what the content will be. Ask: *What do you see here?* When a correct reply is given, have the children find and read the words. Ask children to read page 3 to find out why the polar bear has thick fur.

Pages 4-5: Ask children to check the text and photograph to find out how the bear gets its fur dry after swimming. Read the text together.

When it gets back on land water drips from its fur. It shakes itself to dry its fur.

5

Pages 6-7: Have children read the heading. Ask: *What kind of feathers do you see? How do the long feathers help the bird?* Have children read part of the text to reply.

Think of the animals you know. Which have fur or feathers? Which have scales or skin?

16

Pages 8-15: Continue modeling the structure and content of the book. Encourage children to use a range of problem-solving strategies to check predictions. Does the word look right? Does it sound right? Does it make sense? What letter does it begin with? How do the headings help children to read these pages?

Page 16: Ask children to skim the page silently to see if there are any tricky parts.

Ask children to return to page 2 and read aloud independently. Observe their strategies and behaviors. Can they recognize and read the headings? Are they confident when reading the repetitive introductions? Using known words to help read unfamiliar words?

Rereading and discussing

- Discuss what children liked and what they learned. Return to pages 8 and 9 and discuss how *ph* and *f* each represent the same sound. Have them find the *ph* words on pages 14 and 15.
- Ask children to turn back to the contents page and choose one topic to buddy-read. Observe the reading again.

Science connections

In this activity children will identify the external features of a variety of animals.

Materials: pictures of a variety of animals with fur, feathers, skin, and scales from nature calendars or magazines

- Call on children to name the animals they met in *Fur, Feathers, Scales, Skin* and to identify whether the animal had fur, feathers, skin, or scales. Briefly discuss how having a protective covering helps an animal live in its environment.
- Display pictures of other animals and have children identify the covering of each. If they can, have them tell how the covering helps the animal live in its environment.
- Have children sort the pictures into four groups: animals with fur, animals with feathers, animals with skin, animals with scales.

Reading and writing science

- Have each child make a set of animal trading cards. Have children look through nature magazines or calendars to find four small pictures of animals—one with scales, one with fur, one with feathers, one with skin. Cut sheets of $8\,^1/_2"$ x 11" paper (oak tag is best) into fours for each child. Have children glue a picture of an animal on one side. On the other side have them write the animal's name; whether it has fur, feathers, skin, or scales; and in what kind of habitat it lives—rain forest, desert, woodlands, lake, ocean, mountains, and so on. Provide assistance as necessary. Have children share and talk about their trading cards in small groups.

Cross-curricular activity/math

- Ask children to think about the pets they have at home and whether they have fur, feathers, skin, or scales. Make a simple tally sheet using chart paper. Make and label four columns, one for each skin covering. Tell children that each mark on the tally sheet stands for one pet. Four tally marks with a diagonal line through them equals five pets. Call on children, one at a time, to name their pet(s) and its (their) skin covering. For children who do not have pets, suggest they name a pet they would like to have. Have the child mark one tally line for each pet in the appropriate column. Continue until each child has had a chance. Help children count up the tally marks. Ask questions such as the following, and have children use the data on the tally sheet to answer them: *Which skin covering did most of the pets have? Which skin covering did the least number of pets have? Were there more animals with scales or with fur? Were there more animals with feathers or with skin? How many more?*

Home/school connections

- Encourage children and their families to look for animals in their neighborhood and identify their covering.
- Invite children to take the mini-book home to share with their families.

Non-fiction:

- Brenner, Barbara, and Bernice Chardiet. *Where's That Reptile?* Illustrated by Carol Schwartz. New York: Scholastic, 1995.
- Hirschi, Ron. *Where Are My Bears?* Photos by Erwin and Peggy Bauer. New York: Bantam, 1992.
- Patent, Dorothy Hinshaw. *Bold & Bright Black-and-White Animals.* Illustrated by Kendahl Jan Jubb. New York: Walker, 1998.
- Royston, Angela. *Slinky Scaly Snakes.* New York: DK Publishing, 1998.

Fiction:

- Cannon, Jannell. *Verdi.* San Diego: Harcourt, 1997.
- Deedy, Carmen Agra. *Agatha's Feather Bed.* Illustrated by Laura Seely. Atlanta: Peachtree, 1991.
- Ehlert, Lois. *Feathers for Lunch.* San Diego: Harcourt, 1989.

Let's Bake   B

Standards
Abilities of technological design

Structures and properties of matter

Benchmarks
Tools are used to help make things, and some things cannot be made without tools. Each kind of tool has a special use.

Things can be done to materials to change some of their properties, but not all materials respond the same way.

Supports
- strong photo/text match
- some repetitive language

Challenges
- specialized vocabulary: *mash, measure, pour*
- variety of sentence structures

Text features
Punctuation: quotation marks

High-frequency words: *are, these, they, here, what, like, use, other, will, then, said*

Digraphs: *ch, ck, sh*

Compound words: *teaspoon, everything*

Introducing the text
- Challenge the children to read the title. Focus briefly on the apostrophe.
- Discuss the cover photographs. Draw on children's prior experiences to discuss what kinds of foods are baked in an oven and what the boy might bake using those ingredients and tools.

The first reading

Title page: Read the title page together. Discuss how the tools are used.

Pages 2-3: Have children find and read the words that show what Grandma is going to make. Speculate about the things she will need to do to make banana bread.

Pages 4-5: Confirm the text on page 4. Model some of the ingredients by asking what quantity the recipe asks for.

She says we can use them to make banana bread.

Pages 6-9: Ask: *Why does Grandma need these tools?*

Pages 10-16: Continue to talk about the photographs and text to help children discover information that will support their independent reading. Draw attention to the structure of the text and how this sequencing provides a framework for reading and understanding the book.

We pour the batter into the pan. Now the bread will bake.

Observe the children as they read. Are they self-correcting? Reading with fluent phrasing? Maintaining a focus on meaning? When you are sure that the children have enough information to read the book independently, ask them to return to the front cover and read it themselves.

Rereading and discussing

- Discuss responses to the book. What questions do they have? What helped them successfully read the book? Have the children look at pages 10-14 and model how the writer has used particular words to indicate the sequence *(then, next, last, now)*.
- Observe as they read their books independently or with a buddy. Provide opportunities for them to read the book several times over the next few days.

Science connections

In this activity children will bake banana bread to see how materials change their properties.

Materials: flour, sugar, three ripe bananas, baking powder, salt, 2 eggs, walnuts, bread pan, bowl, mixing spoon, fork

Note: If any child in your class is allergic to nuts, prepare the recipe without the nuts.

Preparation: Before conducting this activity, assemble the ingredients and write the recipe on a large chart. Arrange to bake the bread in the cafeteria or another location in the school.

- Discuss with children what the boy and his grandmother made in *Let's Bake.* Ask them to name some of the ingredients that went into the banana bread and describe the steps that the boy and his grandmother followed. Tell children that they will make their own banana bread to see for themselves how ingredients can change when they are mixed together and baked.
- Assemble all the ingredients at a worktable. Grease the bread pan or use a non-stick pan. Ask two or three children at a time to add one of the ingredients and mix. Have children pay special attention to the amount of each ingredient that is being measured and added and how it changes when it is mixed with the other ingredients. When the batter is ready, pour it into the pan and bake.
- When the bread is baked and cool, cut a small piece for each child.

Reading and writing science

- Create a word web that includes the names of the tools, foods, and action words associated with baking. Begin by having children think of the ingredients, tools, and action words they read about in *Let's Bake*. Then have children write additional words in the web.

Cross-curricular activity/art

Materials: salt, flour, mixing bowls, measuring cups, spoons, small amount of water

- Cover desks or worktables with newspaper.
- Have children work in groups. Provide each group with a mixing bowl, measuring cup, and spoon. Have children carefully measure two cups of flour and two cups of salt, and put them in the bowl. Instruct them to stir the ingredients to mix. Add a half cup of water to the bowl, and have children mix. Continue to add small amounts of water until the mixture is of claylike consistency. Knead the clay once or twice, and divide it among the children in the group.
- Have the children use the clay to create an animal or object of their choice. Allow items to dry for 24 hours. Children can then paint them. Put the items on display, and allow children to view each other's work.

Home/school connections

- Encourage children and their families to create a favorite dish together. Have children share their cooking experience with the rest of the class. Children should be encouraged to name the dish, the ingredients that went into the dish, and what they did for each step.
- Invite children to take the mini-book home to share with their families.

Non-fiction:

- Beech, Linda. *The Magic School Bus Gets Baked in a Cake*. New York: Scholastic, 1995.
- Kazen, Mollie. *Pretend Soup*. Berkeley, CA: Triangle Press, 1994.
- Morris, Ann. *Bread, Bread, Bread*. Photographs by Ken Heyman. New York: Greenwillow, 1989.
- Trumbauer, Lisa. *What Is Matter?* New York: Newbridge Educational Publishing, 1997.

Fiction:

- Carle, Eric. *Walter the Baker*. New York: Simon & Schuster, 1995.
- Hutchins, Pat. *The Doorbell Rang*. New York: Greenwilllow, 1986.
- Soto, Gary. *Too Many Tamales*. Illustrated by Ed Martinez. New York: Putnam, 1993.
- Wing, Natasha. *Jalapeño Bagels*. New York: Atheneum, 1996.

Light and Shadow

Standards
There are several common sources of light, including artificial light and sunlight

Benchmarks
The sun applies heat and light to the earth. Electricity in circuits can produce light and heat.

Supports
- some repetitive language
- moderate to strong photo/text match

Challenges
- specialized language

Text features
Punctuation: apostrophe

High-frequency words: *from, these, some, them, her, down, you, his, your*

Compound words: *flashlights, something*

Introducing the text
- Begin by brainstorming the strategies the children use when they read. What are some ways they figure out unfamiliar words? How do they check for meaning?
- Distribute books and challenge children to read the title. Share the strategies they used to do this.
- Support discussion about the cover photographs and the children's experiences with light and shadow.

The first reading

Title page: Read together.

Pages 2-5:   Briefly survey these pages. Prompt children to use prior knowledge and letter/sound relationships to predict and confirm each source of light.

Pages 6-7:   Model the first sentence. Ask: *What does the sun shine through here? What lets light through them? Do the curtains let all the light through? How much light?*

Pages 8-13:   Continue to build a framework for understanding

We can get light from electric lamps.

Pages 14-15: Ask: *What kind of shadow has this small thing made?* Have children point to the words that tell this and read them together.

Page 16: Let children read independently.

This girl's shadow is flat. Her shadow is flat because the ground is flat.

Observe strategies and behaviors. Are children recognizing the same words and phrases in a variety of sentence structures? Analyzing unfamiliar words and checking that they make sense?

Rereading and discussing

- Invite responses to the book. Encourage the children to ask questions about particular photos and text, and to share new things they learned.
- Ask if there were any tricky words or unusual written language patterns. How did they solve them?

Science connections

In this activity children will explore light and shadow.

Materials: flashlight, small pieces of: clear plastic wrap, clear plastic bag, wax paper, sheer fabric, construction paper, brown paper bag

- Ask children to recall what they read in *Light and Shadow*. Ask them to name some of the sources of light they read about. Write their responses on the chalkboard. Ask volunteers to give examples of when they might use each source of light listed.
- Remind children that in *Light and Shadow* they read that light can shine through some things. Some things let only a little light through, and other things let no light through at all. Display the flashlight and the materials listed above. Tell children you will experiment to see how much light passes through each item. On poster paper make a chart with four columns. Head each column "Items," "All Light," "Some Light," and "No Light." List the items in the first column. Display the items and have children predict whether all, some, or no light will shine through each item. Write their predictions in the appropriate columns.
- Ask a volunteer to hold the flashlight and shine it through each of the items. It is best to shine it against a large sheet of dark paper so that children can easily see how much light is shining through. Have children compare the results with their predictions.

Reading and writing science

- Talk with children about the different shapes shadows can take. Have them name some of the different shapes. You may suggest *flat, bent, long,* or *short*, if children do not think of these words

themselves. Write each word on a strip of paper and display near the science center. Have children look through magazines to find pictures that show shadows. Have them cut out and label the pictures. Each day have several children show their shadow pictures. Display the pictures by the headings.
- Select several poems for children with the themes of light and shadow. Read the poems aloud and invite children to illustrate one of them. Collect the poems in a book and display in the classroom reading center, where children can enjoy them during their independent and small-group work.

Cross-curricular activity/music
- Obtain the words and music for songs that have sun, light, or shadow in their titles, such as *Mister Sun*, *This Little Light of Mine*, and *You Are My Sunshine*. Teach the songs to the children. Have children sing the songs in a light-and-shadow concert that they perform for another class.

Home/school connections
- Encourage children and their families to find one item that lets light shine completely through it, one that lets some light shine through it, and one that lets no light shine through it. Have children make a list of these items and share it with the group.
- Invite children to take the mini-book home to share with their families.

Non-fiction:
- Berger, Melvin. *Light.* New York: Newbridge Educational Publishing, 1992.
- Bulla, Cyde Robert. *What Makes a Shadow?* (rev. ed.) Illustrated by June Otani. New York: HarperCollins, 1994.
- Dodd, Ann Wescott. *Footprints and Shadows*. Illustrated by Henri Sorensen. New York: Aladdin, 1994.
- Goor, Ron and Nancy. *Shadows: Here, There, and Everywhere*. New York: HarperCollins, 1981.

Fiction and poetry:
- Asch, Frank. *Bear Shadow.* New York: Simon & Schuster, 1988.
- Cendrars, Blaise. *Shadow*. Illustrated by Marcia Brown. New York: Aladdin, 1984.
- Keats, Ezra Jack. *Dreams*. New York: Simon & Schuster, 1992.
- Kroll, Steven. *It's Groundhog Day!* Illustrated by Jeni Bassett. New York: Scholastic, 1991.
- Stevenson, Robert Louis. *My Shadow*. Illustrated by Ted Rand. New York: Putnam, 1996.

Our Senses
B

Standards
Characteristics of organisms

Benchmarks
People use their senses to find out about their surroundings and themselves.

Different senses give different information.

Supports
- familiar experiences
- some repetitive language and text structures

Challenges
- varied print placement
- specialized language: *whoosh*

Text features
Punctuation: question mark

High-frequency words: *many, what, you, things, today, friends, use, feel, wet*

Blends: *br, fr, pl, sk, sm, st, sw*

Introducing the text
- Distribute the books to small groups.
- Tell children the book is called *Our Senses*. Draw on their prior experiences to discuss what these are. Which senses can they see being used in the cover photographs?

The first reading

Title page: Read the title page together. Discuss which senses the boys are using.

Pages 2–3: As you discuss the photographs together, establish the sense. Ask what the boy is telling about his eyes. Model the repetitive language patterns.

Pages 4–5: Continue to establish sense and pattern. Ask what this boy is saying he uses to hear. After a correct response, model *I can hear many things*. Ask what he can hear. Encourage children to read this themselves, checking information in the photographs and print.

I use my nose to smell.
I can smell many things.
6

Page 6: Say: *I use my ...* Have children read the new word and complete the sentence.

Page 7: Ask children to find and read the words that tell what the girl can smell.

Pages 8-16: Briefly survey the photographs and text, introducing unfamiliar words through discussion. Encourage children to use different ways to check predictions. Does it sound right? Does it make sense? Is that the beginning letter children expected to see?

When I play I hear my music. I use other senses, too. I feel and see the guitar.

Ask children to read aloud independently, at their own pace. Observe individual children. Are they cross-checking photographs and print? Are they using multiple strategies to figure out unknown words? Are they using repetitive patterns to maintain momentum?

Rereading and discussing

- Share children's responses to the book. What did they like? What did they learn? Did any of the photographs match their own experiences?
- Share the strategies children used to help them read.
- Talk about blends. Ask children to look through the book and identify them.
- Have children read their books again with a buddy.

Science connections

In this activity children will explore their senses of touch and smell.

Materials: 5 small paper cups per group, 5 cotton balls per group, lemon extract, peppermint extract, perfume, garlic clove, onion, 5 plastic bags, sandpaper, piece of velvet or other soft cloth, glass marble, small rock, small sponge, poster board

Preparation: Smell: For each group, scent five cotton balls with each of the fragrant items and place one cottonball in each cup.

Touch: Place the sandpaper, velvet, marble, rock, and sponge in separate bags.

- Divide the class into five groups and have each group label their cups 1 through 5. Choose a recorder for each group. As the group identifies the scent, the recorder notes the cup number and scent on a sheet of paper. Have groups exchange cups and repeat the process.
- Write each group's findings on the chalkboard. Compare the different answers. Ask children to name other similar smelling items or foods.
- Distribute one bag to each group. Have each child touch and describe how each object feels. Have groups exchange bags and repeat the process. Write the name of each object on the

chalkboard. Have children identify how each object felt. Discuss other sensations our skin can feel (hot, cold, wet, dry).

Reading and writing science

- Provide a collection of materials such as flowers, rocks, bells, ice, etc. Using the book *Our Senses* as a reference, ask the children to list the senses. Ask them to examine each material and to list it alongside the senses they used to find out about it.
- Create a word web for the five senses. Call on children to think of words that describe each of the senses, and write their responses in the web. Have children compare the words for each sense. Point out that some words, such as *sweet*, can be used to describe more than one sense.

Cross-curricular activity/social studies

- Explain to children that some people cannot see or cannot hear, but they are able to carry out their everyday activities. Explain that some blind people have guide dogs. Some elevators have recordings that announce each floor to help blind people. Many elevator control panels have braille labels that blind people can read with their fingers. People who cannot hear may also have dogs to help them. Hearing-impaired people can use special telephones that let them send and receive typewritten messages. Obtain books from your local library on guide dogs and dogs that assist the hearing impaired. Place them in the classroom library for children to read in their free time.

Home/school connections

- Have children and their families name one food for each of the following taste categories: salty, sweet, sour, spicy, and bitter. Have children bring in their lists. Make a chart headed by each of the taste categories. Have children write their food name under each.
- Invite children to take the mini-book home to share with their families.

Non-fiction:

- Aliki. *My Five Senses*. New York: HarperCollins, 1989.
- Berger, Melvin. *See, Hear, Touch, Taste, Smell*. New York: Newbridge Educational Publishing, 1993.
- Cole, Joanna. *You Can't Smell a Flower with Your Ear*. Illustrated by Mavis Smith. New York: Grossett & Dunlap, 1994.
- McMillan, Bruce. *Sense Suspense*. New York: Scholastic, 1994.
- Otto, Carolyn. *I Can Tell by Touching*. Illustrated by Nadine Bernard Westcott. New York: HarperCollins, 1994.

Fiction:

- Howard, Elizabeth Fitzgerald. *Mac & Marie & the Train Toss Surprise*. Illustrated by Gail Gordon Carter. New York: Simon & Schuster, 1993.
- Keats, Ezra Jack. *Apt. 3*. New York: Macmillan, 1986.
- Peterson, Jeanne Whitehouse. *I Have a Sister, My Sister Is Deaf*. New York: HarperCollins, 1977.

Recycle It!

Standards
Understands basic concepts about the structure and properties of matter

Benchmarks
Many materials can be recycled and used again, sometimes in different forms.

Supports
- moderate photo/text match
- repetitive language

Challenges
- varied print placement
- sentence continues across two pages

Text features
Punctuation: ellipses, comma

High-frequency words: *many, throw, things, away, again, used, week, comes, street, truck*

Blends: *gl, pl, pr*

Introducing the text
- Give each child a book. Discuss the front- and back-cover photographs.
- Challenge children to figure out and read the title.
- Draw on children's prior knowledge to discuss what recycling is and what can be recycled in their homes and neighborhoods.

The first reading

Title page: Read the title together and briefly talk about the photo.

Pages 2–3: Model the first page and discuss the photo.

Ask: *What can happen to many things that are thrown away?*

Following a correct answer, have children find and read the word *recycled*.

Ask: *What collects them?* Have children identify and read the words *recycling truck*.

Pages 4–7: Ask: *What can you see that people recycle?* Encourage children to check the

Many of the things people throw away can be used again.

	new print on each page carefully to ensure it matches what they say.
Pages 8-11:	Continue to focus discussion on unfamiliar words and the pattern of the text. Ask: *What is being recycled? What is being made from it?*

You can recycle on the playground. How were old tires used here?

Pages 12-13:   Ask: *What recycled material is this house made of?*
Pages 14-16:   Briefly discuss what is being recycled and how.

Observe children as they read their books independently. Are they noticing and reading word endings correctly? Focusing on meaning? Managing multiple lines of print successfully?

Rereading and discussing

- Discuss what new things they found out about recycling and what parts of the book they particularly liked. Were there any tricky words? If so, how did they work them out? Share some of the different strategies children used successfully. Briefly focus on the word endings in *recycle, recycled,* and *recyling*.
- Have children read their books again to themselves or with a buddy.

Science connections

In this activity children will recycle old newspaper to make recycled paper.

Materials: For each group you will need: a bucket, a wooden spoon with a long handle, old newspapers, pieces of wire mesh 1½ feet by 1½ feet (one for each child), water

Preparation: Call on children to bring some of the items listed from home. On the day before the activity, wad the paper into balls and place in the buckets. Fill the buckets with water and allow paper balls to soak overnight.

- Ask children to recall what they read in *Recycle It!* and to name some of the items that can be recycled. Ask them how these things can be used again. Write their responses on the chalkboard. Remind children that in *Recycle It!* a teacher and her class made recycled paper from old newspapers. Tell children they will use old newspapers to make their own recycled paper.
- Before beginning, spread newspapers on the worktables. Drain most of the water from the buckets. Distribute the materials to each group of children.
- Have children use the wooden spoon to mush up the wet newspapers. Each child should have a chance to stir. Children should stir the newspaper until it is a mushy pulp. Divide the pulp among the children. Have them use their hands to spread an even

layer of the pulp on the wire mesh. Caution them not to push down too hard.
- Move the recycled paper to a windowsill where it can dry. When the paper is dry, have children carefully remove it from the wire mesh.

Reading and writing science

- Have children use the recycled paper to write a short letter to a family member, neighbor, or friend. Brainstorm with children what they might say in their letters. Write some of the sentences on the chalkboard so that children may refer to them. Provide children with envelopes and suggest they hand deliver or mail them.

Cross-curricular activity/social studies

- Help children learn about the recycling rules in your community. Before doing the activity, obtain a list of the rules. Discuss with children what items their families recycle. Write each item on the chalkboard. Next to each item write how the item should be prepared for recycling. For example, cans, bottles, and cartons should be rinsed out. Newspapers might need to be bundled and tied or placed in clear plastic bags. Then, have each child bring in one item from home that can be recycled. Call on children to say how each item needs to be prepared for recycling. Have children rinse out cans, bottles, plastic trays, and so on. Have them tie newspapers in bundles. Provide them with recycling bags or bins. Have them place their items in the appropriate bin.

Home/school connections

- Encourage children and their families to make a list of all the items they recycle in one week. Have children bring in their lists. Make a tally chart and have children tally the number of each item they recycled.
- Invite children to take the mini-book home to share with their families.

Non-fiction:

- Berger, Melvin. *Kids for the Earth.* New York: Newbridge Educational Publishing, 1994.
- Brown, Marc and Laurie K. *Dinosaurs to the Rescue!* Boston: Little, Brown, 1992.
- Gibbons, Gail. *Recycle!* Boston: Little, Brown, 1996.
- Robinson, Fay. *Recycle That!* Chicago: Children's Press, 1995.
- Robinson, Fay. *Too Much Trash!* Chicago: Children's Press, 1995.
- Showers, Paul. *Where Does the Garbage Go?* Illustrated by Randy Chewing. New York: HarperTrophy, 1994.

Fiction:

- Gilman, Phoebe. *Something from Nothing.* New York: Scholastic, 1993.
- Rocklin, Joanne. *How Much Is That Guinea Pig in the Window?* Illustrated by Meredith Johnson. New York: Scholastic, 1995.
- Rosen, Michael. *This Is Our House.* Illustrated by Bob Graham. Cambridge, MA: Candlewick, 1996.

Sounds All Around B

Standards
Understands motion and the principles that explain it

Benchmarks
People use their senses to find out about their surroundings and themselves.

Things that make sounds vibrate.

Supports
- repetitive text structure
- moderate photo/text match

Challenges
- descriptive words
- sentence continues across three pages
- variety of sentence structures

Text features
Punctuation: ellipses

High-frequency words: *we, many, make, some, what, through, trees, does, this, they, when, made, that*

Blends: *bl, cl, cr, dr, gr, pl, tr*

Vowels: *oo, ou*

Introducing the text
- Tell the children the name of the book, and ask what they notice about the words *sound* and *around*.
- Discuss the cover photographs. What is the lamb using to make sounds? What is the boy using?
- Talk about sounds children hear in their homes and neighborhoods and ways they use their own voices to make sounds.

The first reading

Title page: Read together. Invite comments on the sound the fire engine would make.

Pages 2–5: Survey the photographs. Have the class predict how the children in the photos are saying they can use their voices. Encourage them to use print details to confirm.

Pages 6–7: Have the children find and read the sounds each animal makes.

Pages 8–11: Continue guiding the children to notice details in the

We can use our voices to cheer.   3

Page 12:	photographs and text and to focus on their meaning. Prompt them to figure out unfamiliar words for themselves using a variety of effective strategies.
	Model the first line, and challenge the children to find and read the words that tell how people make music.
Pages 13-16:	Ask children to look briefly at these pages to see whether there are any challenging parts. Encourage them to share strategies to solve them.

Lightning cracks and thunder booms. What other sounds does weather make?

9

When you are sure that children have enough information to read the book independently, ask them to return to the front of the book and read it themselves. Observe as children read their books aloud independently. Are they rereading to confirm what they've read or to problem-solve? Remembering to use the repetitive language patterns to maintain meaning and momentum? Self-correcting? Using effective strategies to figure out descriptive words?

Rereading and discussing

- Invite responses to the book and comment positively on strategic behaviors you observed. Ask children to share their strategies for decoding some of the unusual descriptive words.
- Encourage them to read the book again with a friend, each taking turns to read a page.
- Provide opportunities for the children to read the book again over the next several days.

Science connections

In this activity children will see that things that make sounds vibrate.

Materials: For each group of five children you will need: a large button with two holes and a piece of strong thread about 2 feet long

Preparation: String the thread through the holes and tie with a strong knot to make a loop. Pull the thread so that you have a loop 6 inches long on each side of the button.

- Remind children that in the book they just read, they were introduced to many objects that made sounds. Have children recall some of the objects and the sounds they made. Tell children that when an object makes a sound it vibrates, and that most of the time they cannot see the vibration. Explain that they are going to do an experiment in which they can see the vibration of an object when it makes a sound.
- Display one button with loops of string. Demonstrate by putting your index fingers through the loops and twirling the button around to twist the string. Pull the string in and out. The button

will twirl and create a humming sound. Have children note the vibration of the string.
- Distribute a button with loops of string to small groups of children. Give each child the opportunity of twirling the button, creating the humming sound, and observing the vibration of the string.

Reading and writing science

- Discuss and list with children the sounds that are part of their everyday lives. Talk about how some sounds give them important information. The school dismissal bell, for example, tells them it is time to go home. The ambulance siren tells them, "Watch out! The ambulance is rushing to an emergency!" Call on children to name, and perhaps mimic, other sounds in their neighborhood and explain what each sound means. Pay particular attention to those sounds which signal a warning, such as smoke detectors, fire drill alarms, sirens, bells at railroad crossings, and so on.

Cross-curricular activity/music

- Provide children with a variety of music-making instruments, such as kazoos, maracas, drums, cymbals, tambourines, and castanets. Have children work in small groups to create music with their instruments. Then allow each group to make a music presentation to the class.

Home/school connections

- Encourage children and their families to explore the idea that things that make sounds vibrate. The vibrations of some objects are more obvious than others. Children may be able to feel sound vibrations by putting their hands on or near stereo speakers or other objects. Have children share their findings with the class.
- Invite children to take the mini-book home to share with their families.

Non-fiction:

- Moss, Lloyd. *Zin! Zin! Zin! A Violin.* Illustrated by Marjorie Priceman. New York: Simon & Schuster, 1995.
- Orgill, Roxanne. *If I Only Had a Horn: Young Louis Armstrong.* Illustrated by Leonard Jenkins. Boston: Houghton Mifflin, 1997.
- Showers, Paul. *Ears Are for Hearing.* Illustrated by Holly Keller. New York: HarperCollins, 1990.
- Trumbauer, Lisa. *Sound.* New York: Newbridge Educational Publishing, 1997.

Fiction:

- Bryan, Ashley. *The Story of Lightning and Thunder.* New York: Atheneum, 1993.
- Heo, Yumi. *One Afternoon.* New York: Orchard, 1996.
- Meaderis, Angela Shelf. *The Singing Man.* Illustrated by Teresa Schaffer. New York: Holiday House, 1994.
- Sage, James. *The Little Band.* Illustrated by Keiko Narahashi. New York: Simon & Schuster, 1991.
- Showers, Paul. *The Listening Walk.* Illustrated by Aliki. New York: HarperCollins, 1993.

Stars

Standards
Understands essential ideas about the composition and structure of the universe and the earth's place in it

Benchmarks
There are more stars in the sky than anyone can easily count, but they are not scattered evenly, and they are not all the same in brightness or color.

Supports
- moderate photo/text match
- clear text organization

Challenges
- specialized vocabulary: *group, cluster*
- chart

Text features
High-frequency words: *you, see, night, little, three, named, people, sometimes, use, oil*

Blends: *br, cl, gl, st*

Compound words: *cannot, sometimes*

Introducing the text
- Challenge children to read the title. Draw on their prior experience to brainstorm what they know about stars and what they think they might find out about them in this book.

The first reading

Title page: Read this together.

Pages 2-5: Discuss these pages and prompt children to use a range of strategies to figure out unfamiliar words and to focus on each page's meaning.

Pages 6-7: Read the question and model how to read the information on the chart to answer it.

Pages 8-9: Have children find and read the word that tells what a group of stars is called.

Pages 10-11: Model the first two lines. Ask if the shape reminds children of anything, and have them read the words to check their replies.

Pages 12-15: Continue to build a framework by briefly discussing print, modeling sentence patterns and photo details.

Sometimes you can see stars in a group.
These groups are called clusters.

8

Page 16: Challenge the children to silently read this page and to name the star.

We see this yellow star during the day. It is our sun!
16

When you are confident that children have enough information, ask them to read the book from the beginning, aloud and independently. Observe their behaviors and strategies. Are they using letter/sound information effectively? Monitoring meaning as they read? Working out unfamiliar words and checking whether they look and sound right?

Rereading and discussing

- Invite discussion about their responses to the book and focus on some aspect to make a teaching point. Revisit the chart and investigate how each feature of it contributes to its overall meaning.
- Ask them to read their book with a buddy, each taking turns to read a page.

Science connections

In this activity children will use their observations to draw conclusions about a star's brightness.

Materials: two lamps (no shades) with 25-watt bulbs, an extension cord

- Call on children to talk about the stars they see in the night sky. Ask them if any of the stars they see seem brighter than the others. Ask why they think they look brighter. After children respond, tell them that they will do an experiment to see why some stars appear brighter than others.
- Darken the room and have children stand at the very back. Place both lights next to each other in the very front of the room. Ask children which light seems brighter than the other. (They both appear to have the same brightness.)
- Using the extension cord, move one light to the middle of the room. Ask children which light seems brighter than the other. (The one in the middle of the room.)
- Help children conclude that a star's brightness depends on how far it is from Earth. Stars that appear very bright are closer to Earth; stars that appear dimmer are farther away from Earth.

Reading and writing science

- Many cultures created myths to explain the star patterns we see in the sky. Obtain stories about how the constellations came to be and read them to the children. Call on volunteers to retell the myths. Have children draw pictures illustrating their favorite part of a myth and write a caption for it.
- Provide each child with a piece of black construction paper and five or six white stars or small white circles to represent stars. Have children drop the stars on the paper to form a random

pattern and then glue them down. Ask children to use their imaginations to see what animal, object, or person they can make from their star pattern. Provide children with white chalk or white pencils and have them outline their pattern. Allow children time to show their star pattern to the class and to describe the animal, object, or person they see.

Cross-curricular activity/language arts

- If you have not done so already, introduce children to some of the myths that explain how star patterns of people and animals came to be in the night sky. Have children work in small groups. Give each group one imaginary constellation, such as Big Bear, the Hunter, the Big Dog, the Queen, the King, the Dragon. Ask each group to make up their own myth of how that star pattern got in the sky. Have each group tell their myth to the rest of the class.

Home/school connections

- Encourage children and their families to go outside when it is dark and to look closely at the night sky. Suggest that children look for the three bright stars on the Hunter's belt. They are usually easy to find in the late spring/early summer sky. Have children and their families make a list or draw a picture of what they see.
- Some families may enjoy finding the brightest star, marking where they stood and recording where the star was in the sky; for example, above a big tree, above the TV antenna. Ask them to return to the same spot an hour later and see where the star is. Have children share the information with the group, and challenge them to explain what has happened.
- Invite children to take the mini-book home to share with their families.

Non-fiction:

- Bendick, Jeanne. *Stars*. Brookfield, CT: Millbrook Press, 1991.
- Berger, Melvin. *Out in Space*. New York: Newbridge Educational Publishing, 1995.
- Branley, Franklyn. *The Sky Is Full of Stars*. Illustrated by Felicia Bond. New York: HarperCollins, 1981.
- Gibbons, Gail. *Stargazers*. New York: Holiday House, 1991.
- Mitton, Jacqueline. *Zoo in the Sky: A Book of Animal Constellations*. Illustrated by Christina Balit. Washington, DC: National Geographic Society, 1998.

Fiction:

- Goble, Paul. *Her Seven Brothers*. New York: Simon & Schuster, 1993.
- Hort, Lenny. *How Many Stars Are in the Sky?* Illustrated by James Ransome. New York: Morrow, 1991.
- Newman, Leslea. *Too Far Away to Touch*. Illustrated by Catherine Stock. New York: Clarion, 1995.

Taking Care of Baby   B

Standards
Characteristics of organisms

Benchmarks
Living things are found almost everywhere in the world. There are different kinds of living things in different places.

Supports
- repetitive introductory sentence
- headings

Challenges
- specialized vocabulary: *meerkats, sea turtles*
- contents page

Text features
Punctuation: question mark

High-frequency words: *care, who, take, these, bring, they, each, while, ride, look, help*

Blends: *br*

Digraphs: *ch, bh, wh*

Introducing the text
- Brainstorm strategies children will use to help them read.
- Prompt children to read the title independently. Have them describe strategies they used to read unknown words.
- Brainstorm animal babies and who takes care of them. What do the caregivers need to provide?

The first reading

Contents page: Read the title together before discussing the contents page and reading the animals' names. Choose one animal and use the contents information to find it in the book. Note the headings in dark type and how this helps the reader. Use the contents page again to find which animal children will read about first in the book.

Pages 2-3: Read the heading together. Model the page 2 question. Have children silently read page 3 to find the answer. Ask why the fox made the den. Have children find and read the words that tell why.

Its mother takes care of this baby. She carries the baby in her pouch.

5

Pages 4-13: Survey these pages, briefly modeling how to use a range of strategies to deal with unfamiliar words and sentence structures.

Pages 14-16: Challenge children to think how this baby might be different from the others before reading the last page to find out.

Elephants travel in herds. All the bigger elephants help take care of this baby.

When you are satisfied that children have sufficient information to read the books independently, ask them to begin to read aloud from page 2. Observe their behavior and strategies. Are they reading the headings? Recognizing the repetitive question-and-answer format? Noticing changes in syntax? Using effective strategies to figure out unknown words?

Rereading and discussing

- Invite the children's responses to the book. What did they learn? What did they like? Did they try out any new strategies? Praise the effective strategies you observed.
- Ask each child to use the contents page to select two animals to read about to a friend. Provide opportunities for children to read the books again over the next few days.

Science connections

In this activity children will explore different habitats and the animals that live in them.

Materials: Various pictures of animals in their habitats (try to obtain pictures of at least four animals for each habitat). Choose three or four habitats to focus on, such as the rain forest, the desert, the woodlands, the swamp.

- Ask children to tell about some of the animals they met in *Taking Care of Baby*. Then have them describe the places where the various animals lived. Tell children that animals are found throughout the world, but that different kinds of animals live in different places.
- Display a picture of a desert animal and name it. Ask children what they know about a desert, and write their responses on the chalkboard. Point out to children that a desert is a dry region that gets little rainfall. Deserts are often very hot. Some deserts are sandy and have few plants. Display pictures of other desert animals and help children to name them.
- Continue in this manner with several other habitats. Call on children to name other animals that might live in these habitats.
- Provide children with nature magazines and calendars. Ask them to look through the materials to find a picture of an animal from one of the habitats that they have learned about.
- Create a bulletin-board display with sections labeled with the

names of different habitats. Have children show their pictures and tell in which habitat their animal belongs. Have them attach their pictures in the appropriate place on the bulletin board.

Reading and writing science

- Have children complete a word web by sorting the animals in the book into "care categories" such as: *Mother, Mother and Father, Two Mothers, A Baby-Sitter, A Herd,* and *Itself.*
- Have children write animal riddles. Ask them to think of descriptive clues for animals, and write pattern sentences based on their responses. For example: This animal has _____ skin; this animal eats _____; this animal lives in the _____.
- Have each child secretly write the name of an animal on one side of a large index card. Using the pattern sentences, have each child write three clues for their animal on the other side of the card. Divide the class into two teams. Have each team member read his or her clues to the other team, alternating turns between teams. Each correct answer scores one point. High score wins.

Cross-curricular activity/geography

- Have children make simple drawings of the following animals: elephant, kangaroo, penguin, polar bear, tiger, wolf, llama, and buffalo. Display a world map, noting the names of the different continents. Ask children where they might find each animal. Have volunteers locate the appropriate continents and tape the animal drawings to the map.

Home/school connections

- Encourage children and their families to look for the variety of animals that live in the areas around their home. Suggest that they discuss how the animals are well adapted to their environment and if these animals live in any other part of the world.
- Invite children to take the mini-book home to share with their families.

Non-fiction:

- Berger, Melvin. *Animals and Their Babies.* New York: Newbridge Educational Publishing, 1996.
- Berger, Melvin. *Look Out for Turtles!* Illustrated by Megan Lloyd. New York: HarperCollins, 1992.
- Dorros, Arthur. *Elephant Families.* New York: HarperCollins, 1995.
- Hirschi, Ron. *Time for Babies.* New York: Cobblehill/Penguin, 1993.
- Ryden, Hope *Joey.* New York: Morrow, 1994.
- Simon, Seymour. *Wild Babies.* New York: HarperCollins, 1998.

Fiction and poetry:

- Cannon, Janell. *Stellaluna.* San Diego: Harcourt, 1993.
- Conrad, Pam. *Animal Lullabies.* New York: HarperCollins, 1997.
- James, Ellen Foley. *Little Bull: Growing Up on Africa's Elephant Kingdom.* New York: Discovery Kids/Sterling, 1998.

Watching the Weather

Standards
Changes in environments

Changes in earth and sky

Benchmarks
Some events in nature have a repeating pattern.

Supports
- repetitive language patterns
- moderate photo/text match

Challenges
- contents page
- variety of sentence structures

Text features
High-frequency words: *we, very, are, snow, now, not, ground, grow, hot*

Blends: *bl, fl, gr, sn, sp, tr*

Introducing the text
- Tell children the book is called *Watching the Weather*. Read the title together and discuss the cover photographs.
- Draw on their experiences to compare hot summer weather with the other seasons. Conclude the discussion by focusing on how the weather affects what they do and how temperature is measured.

The first reading

Contents page: Read the title together, then have children use the photo clues to read the contents. Model how to use the contents page by choosing one entry and using the page number to locate it and check the heading.

Pages 2–3: Read the heading together. Ask children to look at the photographs to see how they can tell that the weather is getting cool. Model how to read the temperature.

Pages 4–5: Read the first line and ask children what the photographs show. Help them check their predictions. Have all children read the temperature together.

Pages 6–9: Ask children how they know it is cold.

Winter Weather

We are watching the weather.
It is cold.
We can see ice and snow.

Pages 10–15: Continue to briefly survey details in the text and photographs to establish the structure of the text. Encourage children to try out a range of strategies to search, check, and confirm.

Page 16: Model how to read the chart.

Summer Weather

We are watching the weather. It is sunny and very hot.

When you are satisfied that the children have enough information to read the book independently, ask them to return to the front of the book and read it themselves. Observe their behaviors and strategies. Are they cross-checking? Focusing on meaning? Self-correcting soon after a miscue? Provide support for independent reading where necessary.

Rereading and discussing

- Invite responses to the book. In what ways are children's own experiences with seasonal weather similar and different? What do they enjoy doing in hot weather? In cold weather? Focus briefly on a teaching point or talk about a particular strategy that someone has used effectively. Have children read the books again with a partner or by themselves.

Science connections

In this activity children will use a thermometer to record the daily temperature.

Materials: an outdoor thermometer

- Ask children to recall what they read in *Watching the Weather* and to tell what they learned about the various seasons. Ask children to name the season they are experiencing at the present time. Talk about the clothing they wear and what kind of weather they should expect.
- Tell children that scientists read and record the temperature each day. Because they have been doing this for many years, they can see a pattern in the temperature. They know what the temperature is likely to be on a certain day of the year. Write the average temperature for your area for this time of year on the chalkboard. Explain to children that this is what the temperature is likely to be.
- Display the thermometer. Show children how to read the temperature. Tell them they will use the thermometer to read and record the temperature each day. Place the thermometer outside the classroom window. Place a chart or calendar near the thermometer so that children can record the temperature. Ask a volunteer each day to read and record the temperature. Have children compare the temperature with the average temperature for your area, as well as with the previous day's temperature.

Reading and writing science

- Create a word web for the four seasons. Write the names of the four seasons on chart paper. Point to one of the seasons and ask children to think of words that describe the weather for that season. Ask children to think of clothing they might use during that season and activities they might do. Write their responses in the web. Repeat for the remaining seasons. When you are finished, ask children what weather conditions, clothing, and activities some seasons share. For example, it could rain during all four seasons. Have them write words for these similarities.

Cross-curricular activity/art

Materials: construction paper, crayons, paintbrushes, glue, cornmeal, newspapers

- Tell children they are going to make snow pictures. Spread newspapers on desks. Distribute construction paper and crayons to children. Have children draw a winter scene without snow.
- Draw a simple picture of a house and a tree. Using a paintbrush, brush a small amount of glue on the areas of the picture where you would like to have snow. Sprinkle cornmeal on the areas of the picture that have the glue. Move the paper so that cornmeal covers all the areas where you have applied the glue. Shake the excess cornmeal into the trash. Have children add snow to their pictures. Provide help when necessary. Display children's work on the bulletin board.

Home/school connections

- Encourage children and their families to talk about the weather each day and, if possible, to take daily temperature readings. Have families look for and note signs of seasonal changes.
- Invite children to take the mini-book home to share with their families.

Non-fiction:

- Berger, Melvin. *Who Cares about the Weather?* New York: Newbridge Educational Publishing, 1993.
- Hirschi, Ron. *Spring.* New York: Cobblehill, 1990.
- Hutchings, Amy and Richard. *Picking Apples and Pumpkins.* New York: Scholastic, 1994.
- Maas, Robert. *When Winter Comes.* New York: Henry Holt, 1993.

Fiction and poetry:

- Adoff, Arnold. *In for Winter, Out for Spring.* Illustrated by Jerry Pinkney. Orlando: Harcourt, 1991.
- Van Laan, Nancy. *Shingebiss: An Ojibwe Legend.* Illustrated by Betsy Bowen. Boston: Houghton Mifflin, 1997.
- Yolen, Jane. *Weather Report.* Honesdale, PA: Wordsong/Boyds Mills, 1993.

What Do Scientists Do?   B

Standards
Understands the nature of scientific inquiry

Benchmarks
It is important in science to describe things as accurately as possible because it enables people to compare their observations with those of others.

Supports
- moderate photo/text match
- repetitive text structures

Challenges
- sentence continues across two pages
- varied print placement

Text features
Punctuation: ellipses

Blends: *dr, pl*

Digraphs: *ch, ph, th*

Silent *c*

Introducing the text
- Discuss the front- and back-cover photographs. Establish that the children in the photographs are being scientists. Support children as they work out the title for themselves.
- Draw on children's prior experiences to brainstorm a list of things scientists do in order to ask and answer questions. Close the discussion by listing ways that the children are scientists, too.

The first reading

Title page: Invite children to read the title and talk about the photograph. Point out the silent *c* in *scientists*.

Pages 2–5: Ask children to survey the photographs briefly to find out some of the things that scientists do. Encourage them to check details in the text to confirm their predictions.

Page 6: Ask children to read to find out why scientists make plans.

Pages 7–8: Discuss why scientists take photographs. Ask how else they record information. Read page 8 together.

Pages 9–15: Briefly survey the photographs, focusing the discussion on

They also make charts to show what they found.

Page 16: what is going on and what the children would say they were doing.

Have children work this page out for themselves and read it together.

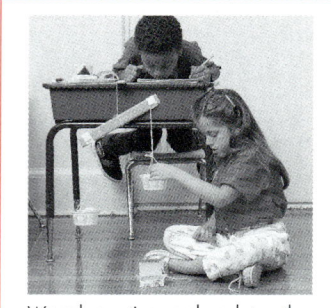

We ask questions and work together to find out answers.

Ask children to turn back to the cover and quietly read the book aloud to themselves, independently. Observe their reading behaviors and strategies. Encourage them to take risks to develop their range of effective strategies. Are they rereading to check and confirm? Are they using print and photographs in an integrated way? Are they recognizing and using the repetitive format of the book to read the second half?

Rereading and discussing

- Invite discussion about children's responses to the book. Remind them that scientists continually ask questions. Then focus on several of the photographs and the questions the scientists might be asking.
- Ask children to reread *What Do Scientists Do?* to a buddy or independently. Provide time for them to reread the text independently during the next few days.

Science connections

In this activity children will explore scientific processes and record their findings.

Materials: a variety of objects from nature, such as rocks, feathers, leaves, and shells; rulers; scales

- Ask children to recall the things that scientists do for ideas. Write their responses on the chalkboard. Explain to children that when they do experiments or study an item they are being scientists, too.
- Choose an item from nature. Hold it up for children to see. Have children describe what it looks like. Make a sketch of it on the chalkboard. Write down the words that children used to describe its texture, color, and any other characteristics. Have a volunteer use a ruler to measure the item. Record its length on the chalkboard. Have a volunteer use a scale to weigh the item. Record its weight on the chalkboard. Tell children that they will now work with a partner to investigate their own item.
- Distribute items to partners. Have partners carefully examine the item. Have them draw a picture of the item and write down words that describe it. Have children use rulers and scales to measure, weigh, and record data. Provide assistance as necessary.
- Allow partners time to share their findings with the rest of the class. Have children with items of the same category (for example, all children with shells) compare their findings.

Reading and writing science

- Write "I am a scientist" on the chalkboard. Have children think of a time when they felt like scientists. Call on volunteers to share their experiences. Draw attention to the scientific processes that children mention. Write these sentences on the chalkboard: *I looked and listened. I took notes. I watched how things changed.* Distribute drawing materials to children. Have children write "I am a scientist" at the top of their papers. Then have them draw a picture of an experience in which they felt like a scientist. Have children write a sentence or two describing their experience. Suggest that they use the model sentences on the chalkboard to help them.

Cross-curricular activity/math

Materials: tape measure, ruler

- Remind children that describing things as accurately as possible is important in science. For example, recording information accurately helps meteorologists predict what the weather will be. Tell children they will take turns measuring and recording their heights. Attach the tape measure to a wall in your classroom. Demonstrate how to measure height. Have a child stand with his or her back to the tape measure. Place a ruler on the child's head so that it is perpendicular to the wall and the back of it touches the tape measure. Have the child move away from the wall and read the tape measure. Show children the correct way to record feet and inches. Have children work in groups to measure and record their heights. Then call on groups to share their results. Make a chart to record results, and have children use the chart to compare their heights.

Home/school connections

- Encourage children to choose an everyday object or event at home and to ask or write questions about it. For example: *Why does toothpaste foam? How do eggs change when they are cooked?* Have children share their questions with the class.
- Invite children to take the mini-book home to share with their families.

Non-fiction:

- Accorsi, William. *Rachel Carson.* New York: Holiday House, 1993.
- Florian, Douglas. *Nature Walk.* New York: Greenwillow, 1989.
- Selsam. Millicent. *How to Be a Nature Detective.* Illustrated by Marlene Hill. New York: HarperCollins, 1995.

Fiction:

- Burns, Marilyn. *How Many Feet? How Many Tails?* New York: Scholastic, 1996.
- Franklin, Kristin. *Iguana Beach.* Illustrated by Lori Lohstoeter. New York: Crown, 1998.
- Leedy, Loreen. *Measuring Penny.* New York: Henry Holt, 1998.

Where Does the Water Go?

Standards
Properties of objects and materials

Changes in earth and sky

Benchmarks
Water left in an open container disappears, but water left in a closed container does not disappear.

Supports
- strong photo/text match

Challenges
- concepts
- specialized language
- diagram

Text features
High-frequency words: *water, go, from, this, get, look, when, you, these, into*

Vowels: *ai, oa*

Compound words: *cannot, sometimes*

Introducing the text
- Focus discussion on the front cover. Challenge children to use known words and punctuation to figure out and read the title. Talk about where the droplets on the stem will go and what happens to puddles when they dry up. Establish that children will not be able to see the water in the air, but there is a way to prove that there is water vapor in the air.
- Set up the experiment on page 111 and tell children you will check it together every day.
- Tell the children the book is about the water cycle. Turn to page 14 and discuss the diagram.

The first reading

Title page: Read this together.

Pages 2-3:   Ask: *What is happening here?* and have children check that their responses match the written text.

Pages 4-5:   Model and briefly discuss the words *water vapor*.

Pages 6-7:   Have the children find the words *water vapor* on these pages.

Pages 8-9: Ask them to find what clouds are made of. Recall the diagram of the water cycle and discuss why the clouds are getting bigger.

Water vapor changes back into water. When it is cold, it can fall as snow.

Pages 10-13: Continue discussing the sequence of events, drawing on a range of strategies to help children figure out sentence structures and unfamiliar vocabulary.

Pages 14-15: Briefly revisit the water cycle diagram.

Page 16: Show children how to use the index.

Invite children to read their books aloud, but independently of others. Observe their strategies and behaviors. Are they recognizing and reading high-frequency words? Using known words to figure out unknown words? Self-correcting?

Rereading and discussing

- Invite responses to the book. What interested children the most? What questions do they have? Ask them to identify tricky words or tricky parts of the text.
- Have children discuss effective strategies for solving problems with the text. Ask them to reread their books independently or with a buddy. When they have finished, give them time to work together and to practice using the index or reading the diagram.

Science connections

In this activity children will observe that water in an open container is absorbed into the air and that water in a closed container is not absorbed.

Materials: 2 glasses, water, watercolor paint, a plate

- Discuss with children what they learned in *Where Does the Water Go?* Review the water cycle with them by posing questions such as, "When it rains we sometimes see puddles on the ground. What happens to the puddles when the sun comes out? Where does the water go?" Tell children that they will do an experiment to discover whether or not water is absorbed into the air.
- Have children fill two glasses each with the same amount of water. You may want to color the water with a little bit of watercolor paint to make it easy to see. Have children cover the top of one glass with a plate. Put both glasses on the windowsill in the sun.
- Each day, call children's attention to the glasses. Have them use a ruler to measure the amount of water in each glass. By day three or four a significant amount of water should have evaporated from the uncovered glass. Help children conclude that the water in the uncovered glass was absorbed by the air. The water in the other glass could not be absorbed because the glass was covered.

Reading and writing science

- Have children look through magazines to find and cut out pictures of a rainy or cloudy day. Have children paste their pictures onto sheets of construction paper. Tell children you would like each of them to write a sentence describing their picture. Brainstorm with children to come up with some words they might like to use. Write these on a chart. Encourage children to use the book as a reference, as well. Allow time for children to present their pictures to the class and to read their sentences.

Cross-curricular activity/art

- Conduct this activity in the school playground. Provide each child with a paintbrush and a cup of water. Have each child find a spot on the playground and paint a picture using the water. Give children the opportunity to look at each other's artwork and to notice what happens to the "paintings." Help children conclude that the water used to make their pictures was absorbed into the air.

Home/school connections

- Have children and their families keep a log of instances when water turns into water vapor or steam. Suggest they notice a steamy shower or bath, steam coming from a teakettle, steam from a steam iron, and so on. Allow children time to share their findings with the rest of the class. Keep a classroom log where you can record children's responses.
- Invite children to take the mini-book home to share with their families.

Non-fiction:

- Asch, Frank. *Water.* San Diego: Harcourt, 1995.
- Berger, Melvin. *Amazing Water.* New York: Newbridge Educational Publishing, 1996.
- Branley, Franklyn. *Rain and Hail.* Illustrated by Harriet Barton. New York: Harper Collins, 1983.
- Cole, Joanna. *The Magic School Bus Gets Wet All Over.* New York: Scholastic, 1996.
- Fowler, Alan. *The Earth Is Mostly Ocean.* Chicago: Children's Press, 1993.
- Peters, Lisa Westberg. *Water's Way.* Illustrated by Ted Rand. Boston: Little, Brown, 1991.

Fiction:

- Keats, Ezra Jack. *A Snowy Day.* New York: Puffin, 1976.
- Lee, Huy Voun. *In the Snow.* New York: Henry Holt, 1995.
- Medearis, Angela Shelf. *We Play on a Rainy Day.* New York: Scholastic, 1993.
- Serfozo, Mary. *Rain Talk.* Illustrated by Keiko Narahashi. New York: Simon & Schuster, 1993.
- Shaw, Charles G. *It Looked Like Spilt Milk.* New York: HarperCollins, 1992.

Photo Credits

Introduction

Cover: Johnny Johnson/DRK Photo; Title Page: Stephen Ogilvy; Page 3: (top) H. Richard Johnston/FPG International; (bottom) Nora & Rick Bowers/The Wildlife Collection; Page 5: M.J. Manuel/Photo Researchers, Inc.; Page 6: Marc Epstein/DRK Photo; Page 7: Stephen Ogilvy; Page 8: (top left) Leonard Lee Rue/Animals Animals; (top right) Nora & Rick Bowers/The Wildlife Collection; (bottom left) Marc Epstein/DRK Photo; (bottom right) James Rod/Photo Researchers, Inc; Page 9: (top left) Neil Ricklen/PhotoEdit; (top right) Alan Oddie/PhotoEdit; (bottom left) David Pollack/The Stock Market; (bottom right, left) Renee Lynn/Photo Researchers, Inc.; (bottom right, right) Renee Lynn/Photo Researchers, Inc.; Page 10: (top left) Sue Pashko/Envision; (top right) Coco McCoy/Rainbow; (bottom) Gerard Lacz/Animals Animals; Page 11: (top left and top right) Stephen Ogilvy; (center left) David Nunuk/ Science Photo Library/Photo Researchers, Inc.; (center right) John Chumack/Photo Researchers, Inc.; (bottom) Carl Purcell/Photo Researchers, Inc.; Page 12: (top) Copyright 1998 PhotoDisc, Inc.; (center left) Aaron Haupt/Photo Researchers, Inc.; (center right) Debrah Welling; Page 13: (top left and top right) Stephen Ogilvy; (center left) Steve Kaufman/DRK Photo; (center right) Partridge Osf/Animals Animals/Earth Scenes; (bottom left) William H. Mullins/Photo Researchers, Inc.; (bottom right) Alan D. Carey/Photo Researchers, Inc.; Page 14: Brian Kenney/ Masterfile; Page 15: Stephen Ogilvy; Page 16: Stephen Ogilvy

Set A

Animals From Long Ago: Page 2: Neg. No. K17197, Photo by Denis Finnin, Courtesy Dept. of Library Services, American Museum of Natural History, NY; Page 13: Neg. No. 5493(2), Courtesy Dept. of Library Services, American Museum of Natural History, NY; *Animal Messengers*: Page 4: © 1998 PhotoDisk, Inc.; Page 14: Roy Morsch/The Stock Market; *At the Playground*: Page 5: Jim Cummins/FPG International; Page 14: (left) Martin Rogers/Tony Stone Images, (right) Michael Hart/FPG International; *Beaks*: Page 3: C. Allan Morgan/Peter Arnold, Inc.; Page 16: Ralph A. Reinhold/Animals Animals; *Bikes*: Page 5: Myrleen Ferguson/PhotoEdit; Page 14: Dana White/PhotoEdit; *City Buildings*: Page 5: James Black/The Stock Market; Page 13: Lawrence Migdale/ Photo Researchers, Inc.; *Day and Night*: Page 4: Stephanie Rausser/FPG International; Page 12: Bill Bachman/Photo Researchers, Inc.; *How Animals Move*: Page 2: Stephen Dalton/Photo Researchers, Inc.; Page 12: Gerard Lacz/Animals Animals; *Kittens*: Page 4: Bob Schwartz; Page 10: Norvia Behling/Behling & Johnson; *Let's Make Something New*: Page 6: Stephen Ogilvy; Page 16: Stephen Ogilvy; *Rocks*: Page 5: Tom Till Photography; Page 12: Henry H. Holdsworth/The Wildlife Collection; *Snails in School!*: Page 2: Stephen Ogilvy; Page 12: Stephen Ogilvy; *Up Close*: Page 6: Tom McHugh/Photo Researchers, Inc.; Page 11: David Woods/The Stock Market; *What Can Change?*: Page 3: Don Mason/The Stock Market; Page 11: Paula Lerner/The Picture Cube; *What Does a Garden Need?*: Page 3: Marc Romanelli/The Image Bank; Page 11: Pete Saloutos/The Stock Market; *Where Are the Eggs?*: Page 2: Robert Maier/Animals Animals; Page 15: Art Wolfe/Tony Stone Images

Set B

Animals Build: Page 2: Robert Lankinen/The Wildlife Collection; Page 15: Larry Ulrich/DRK Photo; *At the Science Center*: Page 4: Stephen Ogilvy; Page 10: Stephen Ogilvy; *The Coral Reef*: Page 5: Larry Lipsky/Bruce Coleman, Inc.; Page 16: Norbert Wu Photography; *Corn: From Farm to Table*: Page 7: SuperStock; Page 10: Lowell J. Georgia/Photo Researchers, Inc.; *From the Earth*: Page 3: Bruce M. Wellman/Stock Boston; Page 11: Index Stock Photography, Inc.; *Fur, Feathers, Scales, Skin*: Page 5: Tom & Pat Leeson/DRK Photo; Page 16: Tom & Dee Ann McCarthy/The Stock Market; *Let's Bake*: Page 3: Stephen Ogilvy; Page 14: Stephen Ogilvy; *Light and Shadow*: Page 4: Dale Guldan/The Picture Cube; Page 12: Jerry Koontz/The Picture Cube; *Our Senses*: Page 6: Peter Steiner/The Stock Market; Page 12: Charles Gupton/The Stock Market; *Recycle It!*: Page 2: Jon Feingersh/The Stock Market; Page 15: Richard Hutchings/PhotoEdit; *Sounds All Around*: Page 3: Ed Bock/The Stock Market; Page 9: Ralph Wetmore/Tony Stone Images; *Stars*: Page 8: David Nunuk/Science Photo Library/Photo Researchers, Inc.; Page 16: Tom Stock/Tony Stone Images; *Taking Care of Baby*: Page 5: L. Villota/Bruce Coleman, Inc.; Page 13: Martin Harvey/The Wildlife Collection; *Watching the Weather*: Page 6: Michael Habicht/Animals Animals; Page 14: Bachmann/Photo Researchers, Inc.; *What Do Scientists Do?* Page 8: David J. Sams/ Stock Boston; Page 14: Richard Hutchings/Photo Researchers, Inc.; *Where Does the Water Go?*: Page 4: Robert Brenner/PhotoEdit; Page 12: D. Cavagnaro/DRK Photo

Standards/Benchmarks

	Title	Standards
Set A	Animals From Long Ago	Characteristics of organisms
	Animal Messengers	Characteristics of organisms
	At the Playground	Position and motion of objects
	Beaks	Knows about the diversity and unity that characterize life
	Bikes	Abilities of technological design
	City Buildings	Understands basic concepts about the structure and properties of matter
	Day and Night	Understands basic features of earth
	How Animals Move	Knows about the diversity and unity that characterize life
	Kittens	Characteristics of organisms
	Let's Make Something New	Structure and properties of matter
	Rocks	Properties of earth materials
	Snails in School!	Characteristics of organisms Organisms and environments
	Up Close	Understands the nature of technological design

Benchmarks

Some kinds of organisms that once lived on earth have completely disappeared although they were similar to others that are alive today.

Information can be sent and received in many different ways.

Things move in different ways, such as straight, zigzag, round and round, back and forth, fast and slow. The way to change how something is moving is to give it a push or a pull.

Animals eat and use other plants and animals.

Most things are made of parts.

Something may not work if some of its parts are missing.

Objects can be described in terms of the materials they are made of and their physical properties—color, size, shape.

The sun can be seen only during the day, but the moon can be seen sometimes at night, and sometimes during the day.

The sun, moon, and stars all appear to move slowly across the sky.

Some animals and plants are alike in the way they look and in the things they do and others are very different from one another.

Things can change in different ways such as size, color, weight, movement. Some small changes can be detected by taking measurements.

Make something out of cardboard, wood, plastic, metal, or existing objects that can be actually used to perform a task.

Chunks of rock come in many sizes and shapes, from boulders to grains of sand and even smaller.

A lot can be learned about plants and animals by observing them closely, but care must be taken to know the needs of living things and how to provide for them in the classroom.

Most living things need water, food, and air.

Magnifiers help people see things they could not see without them.

Sometimes a person can get different information by moving closer or farther away.

Set B

Title	Standards
What Can Change?	Understands basic earth processes
	Understands cycling of matter and flow of energy
What Does a Garden Need?	Knows the general structure and functions of cells in organisms
Where Are the Eggs?	Knows about the diversity and unity that characterize life
Animals Build	Organisms and environments
	Characteristics of organisms
At the Science Center	Understands the nature of scientific inquiry
The Coral Reef	Understands how species depend on one another and the environment for survival
Corn: From Farm to Table	Abilities of technological design
	Characteristics of organisms
From the Earth	Understands energy types, sources, and conversions
Fur, Feathers, Scales, Skin	Understands how species depend on one another and on the environment for survival
Let's Bake	Abilities of technological design
	Structures and properties of matter
Light and Shadow	Changes in the earth and sky
Our Senses	Characteristics of organisms

Benchmarks

Change is something that happens to many things.
Changes happen in everyone's life.

To grow well, plants need warmth, light, and water.

Living things have offspring, usually with two parents involved.

Animals and plants sometimes change their surroundings.

Objects can be described in terms of materials they are made of (clay, cloth, paper, etc.) and their physical properties (color, size, shape, weight, etc.).

People can often learn about things around them by just observing those things carefully, but sometimes they learn more by doing something to these things and noting what happens to them.

Living things are found almost everywhere in the world.

Plants and animals have features that help them live in different environments.

Animals use plants (or even other animals) for shelter and nesting.

Machines improve what people reap from crops—by helping in planting and harvesting, and in transporting it long distances.

People burn fuels such as wood, oil, coal, and natural gas, or use electricity to cook their food and warm their homes.

Different plants and animals have external features that help them thrive in different kinds of places.

Tools are used to help make things and some things cannot be made without tools. Each kind of tool has a special use.

Things can be done to materials to change some of their properties, but not all materials respond the same way.

The sun applies heat and light to the earth.

Electricity in circuits can produce light and heat. There are several common sources of light, including artificial light and sunlight.

People use their senses to find out about their surroundings and themselves. Different senses give different information.

Title	Standards
Recycle It!	Understands basic concepts about the structure and properties of matter
Sounds All Around	Understands motion and the principles that explain it
Stars	Understands essential ideas about the composition and structure of the universe and the earth's place in it
Taking Care of Baby	Characteristics of organisms
Watching the Weather	Changes in environments Changes in the earth and sky
What Do Scientists Do?	Understands the nature of scientific inquiry
Where Does the Water Go?	Properties of objects and materials Changes in the earth and sky

Benchmarks

Many materials can be recycled and used again, sometimes in different forms.

People use their senses to find out about their surroundings and themselves.

Things that make sounds vibrate.

There are more stars in the sky than anyone can easily count, but they are not scattered evenly, and they are not all the same in brightness or color.

Living things are found almost everywhere in the world. There are different kinds in different places.

Some events in nature have a repeating pattern.

It is important in science to describe things as accurately as possible because it enables people to compare their observations with those of others.

Water left in an open container disappears, but water left in a closed container does not disappear.

Standards/Benchmarks reproduced from *Benchmarks for Science Literacy* by American Association for the Advancement of Science. Copyright © 1993 by the American Association for the Advancement of Science. Used by permission of Oxford University Press, Inc.

About the Author

Dr. Brenda Parkes

Dr. Brenda Parkes is a well-known Australian educator and author who has conducted keynote presentations, workshops, and seminars in the United States, Canada, Britain, and Australia. Brenda trained as an early childhood teacher in New Zealand and taught there for some years before moving to Australia. Until recently she was a senior lecturer in Literacy Education at Griffith University.

Brenda has also worked with school districts in the United States and Australia as an on-site literacy consultant for early childhood literacy programs. Her work keeps her in frequent contact with teachers and children in early childhood settings.

Brenda has written many books for shared and guided reading, including the very popular *Who's in the Shed?* and *The Enormous Watermelon*. Currently she is guiding the development and writing of additional titles in the Discovery Links series from Newbridge Educational Publishing.